Chicken Shift for the Soul

A Decade's Worth of Potent Nourishment

Cynthia Barlow

© Copyright 2006 Cynthia Barlow.
All rights reserved. No part of this publication may be reproduced, stored in a retrieval system, or transmitted, in any form or by any means, electronic, mechanical, photocopying, recording, or otherwise, without the written prior permission of the author.

Note for Librarians: A cataloguing record for this book is available from Library and Archives Canada at www.collectionscanada.ca/amicus/index-e.html
ISBN 1-4120-9692-8

Printed in Victoria, BC, Canada. Printed on paper with minimum 30% recycled fibre.
Trafford's print shop runs on "green energy" from solar, wind and other environmentally-friendly power sources.

TRAFFORD
PUBLISHING
Offices in Canada, USA, Ireland and UK

Book sales for North America and international:
Trafford Publishing, 6E–2333 Government St.,
Victoria, BC V8T 4P4 CANADA
phone 250 383 6864 (toll-free 1 888 232 4444)
fax 250 383 6804; email to orders@trafford.com

Book sales in Europe:
Trafford Publishing (UK) Limited, 9 Park End Street, 2nd Floor
Oxford, UK OX1 1HH UNITED KINGDOM
phone 44 (0)1865 722 113 (local rate 0845 230 9601)
facsimile 44 (0)1865 722 868; info.uk@trafford.com

Order online at:
trafford.com/06-1448

10 9 8 7 6 5 4 3 2

Contents

Introduction 1
A Starting Point: Birthing Love 7
Lullaby Lament. 18
On Giving it Your Best Shot 21
Christmas Truths. 24
The Greatest Gift. 26
Hard Choices and Heart Scars 29
An Easter Follow-up 33
Essential Freedoms 37
In Memory of Megan. 41
Trust Your Swing 62
Personal Branding 65
Worry Shadows 68
The Value of Pondering 71
The Price of Perfection. 74
Spring Cleaning and Sisters 77
God Sings For You 82
In the Echoes of Silence 86
Fingerprints on the Ceiling 90
The Day It Rained Cement 94
Sifting Through the Rubble 98

Intangibles: The Stuff of Substance 103
Towers, Truth and Trusting 108
Quiet White Wonders and Love Collisions 111
Trail Markers and Soul Whispers 116
On Holy Ground. 122
Balance Sheets and Creative Accounting 126
Charity from the Inside Out 129
Finding the Soft Spot of Safety. 133
Mountains, Milestones and Memories. 135
Promoting a Platform for Peace 140
Creating Christmas all Year Long 142
Both Sides of Hope. 145
A Mid-point: Mortality Awareness 148
Attics, Sheds and Invincibility 151
Heroes, Eagles and Miracle-Makers 154
Tragedies, Trials and Triumphs 157
Trials Terminated 162
Prisons, Promises and Paradise. 166
One Good Question 169
Sundials, Shining and Sharing. 172
On Family Patterns and Community Living 175
On Landscapes, Leadership and Compasses 178
An Expert Source. 182
Compassion in Crisis. 185
The Ultimate Form of Self-Mastery 188
The Freedom of Dancing with Death 191
Finding the Chuckle Inside 195
Mechanical Dependency. .198
The Point in Between 202
Laws of Life. 204

The World of One 210
A New Paradigm for Performance Improvement 214
Enter In 218
The Value of Transparency. 219
The Weight of Character. 222
In the End: Back to the Beginning. 225
Afterward 247

For Michael and Andrew
my greatest teachers

Chicken Shift for the Soul

Introduction

"Love does not dominate, it cultivates."
—Goethe

THE RETREAT SITE MY COMPANY used to lease for self-development programs was situated near fields that had been farmed for generations. Rich, black soil produced corn, potatoes, lettuce, tomatoes and more. The fields spread out to the horizon, dotted here and there with small enclaves of trees, barns and occasional homes. Cows wandered about congregating at hay feeds, providing ample supplies of fertilizer. On days when the farmers distributed this dried and pungent supply over the fields with tractor driven arms of steel, the aroma floated on the wind for miles.

I was a city gal to these folk, many of whom – most, actually – had lived in this rural area since birth. Their personal lives revolved around the climate cycles; yearly seasons coupled with proper weather conditions determined the daily priorities, so on fertilizing days everyone went about their business without any disruption. If they even noticed the acrid aroma they never complained about it. I, on the other hand, seemed always to be caught slightly off guard; on a perfectly beautiful, crystal clear day in early spring a sickening stench would suddenly assault my nostrils. *Why do they choose to spread manure on such a beautiful day as this when people want to be outside?* Exactly. That's why the farmers are in the fields doing what they're doing, you silly city slicker. It's a *perfect* day to spread manure.

Now, as any local dweller can attest, there are lots of different kinds of manure used for fertilizing: cow, horse, pig and chicken. Almost any kind will add rich nutrients to the soil. Cow manure gets used a lot; horse manure used less, and on *really* special days they roll out the chicken cast-offs. The first time I smelled that smell (it's unforgettable) was at the local gas station where I had stopped at to fill up. Opening the car door, I thought there might be something *terribly* wrong somewhere nearby. I asked the teenage attendant if she knew what the stench was.

"They're spreading manure today," she said.

"Whew! It's potent stuff," I commented. "Smells different than other fertilizing days,"

"Yeah, but it's still shit – just chicken shit today." She started pumping my gas.

"Chicken shit?" I lifted my nose to the air. So *that's* what a chicken farm smells like.

"Yeah. Pretty bad, huh?" She followed my gaze. "Believe it on not, you get used to it after a while. It's actually my dad's farm down the road. The stuff's really good for the soil, but it's so concentrated you can't use it all the time, else it would destroy the crops. It's real strong." She paused as she replaced the nozzle in the gas pump. "But when the wind's movin' it can sure smell like shit around here."

We both chuckled at the apt use of the euphemism and I paid her and left.

Eventually I got used to the smelly days. They're a great metaphor for life. Certain days are just "fertilizing" days. Out of the blue, on an otherwise seemingly normal day, something will happen and suddenly there's a metaphoric stench. Days I deem difficult, unfair or overwhelming are generally days in which I'm being strengthened, nourished or refined. Remembering the promise of future "crops" helps me accept the "aroma" of the inconvenient or painful event. When a smelly day erupts from nowhere I remind myself to:

1. Trust in Mother Nature — She lets you know when the time is right to fertilize.
2. Invest in your Soil — Tilling the earth predetermines the quality of future crops.
3. Acknowledge the Paradox — There's shit on sunny days and there's sun on shitty days.

It may not be true. It may not be right. But it sure does help me when the wind's movin'.

I like to think of it as chicken shit for the soul.

⁓

This volume contains a collection of commentaries accumulated over the past decade. Culled from monthly newsletters sent to clients, students and curious on-lookers of my generally unorthodox, sometimes irreverent and most times self-revealing observations, they chronicle the fertilization process that has help to produce the rich soil of my life. Some personal chicken shit for the soul; insights sprouted from the reflective process required to decompose daily events, shifting do-do into data.

As I sorted and sifted and edited, a theme emerged: the search for an understanding of the nature of love as reflected through relationships, especially the relationships with family, specifically my sons. Quite against my own desires the book morphed into a sort of memoir.

My life has been no more interesting or difficult than most, and a lot less than some. It has, however, seemed to serve as a beacon to a rare few who have told me that the stories I share during workshops and retreats – my analogies and interpretations of why things happen the way they do sometimes – have helped them to untangle their own emotional wiring. I use personal examples of the concepts I teach because it helps *me* untangle as well! I try to make sense of things because, basically, I've found life to be a rather baffling sort of experience. Rich and rewarding to be sure, but somewhat like shooting rapids on a long river. It can become tiring and confusing indeed. Yet, it is a remarkable ride worth the effort required to navigate the maelstroms and messy moments inherent to living.

Everyone needs a beacon to steer them from unnoted shores and unseen shoals. I wrote these observations as a way to support and maintain contact with clients and friends, who often forward them on to others. Much to my amazement, over the years I've heard from people scattered across the globe. May this book travel as widely.

As a direct result of Harvard professor Harry G. Frankfurt's recent New York Times bestseller, *On Bullshit*, I dared to include so coarse a word as "shit" in the title. While I recognize that there may be some people who could recoil (if you're one of them, get over it), I have rarely backed down in the face of potential confrontation. And while the term "chicken shit" has developed a rather derogatory connotation, the word itself is fairly main stream these days and the euphemistic implications dovetail nicely with the intent of this volume: to both strengthen and nourish one's spirit by shifting one's focus.

I had reason to require both this past year as I compiled and corrected my previous columns: my husband and I barely escaped death in March 2005 due to a carbon-monoxide leak in our home. We lay unconscious for several days before being rescued. Since I write about that experience herein I will not go into details now. Suffice it to say that the road to recovery has been a steep climb since that event. Certain things have fallen into place, even as some previous priorities have slipped from my plate. Much has altered, both inside and out.

Recently, after making some final corrections to the manuscript, I had reason to re-read my own words: I was in a low place, questioning my value, doubting the climb, wondering if this thing called life was *really* worth the effort. I don't get those days often. But this day was a doozey as my mother would say, and I am pleased and strangely humbled to be able to say that I was both comforted and strengthened by what I read that day. In fact, my own words – so far removed from my immediate experience at that moment – melted the iceberg of fear I felt in my heart that particular day. This gives me courage to commit this collection to print in a frozen format and offer you, the reader, not platitudes but fresh perspectives that may help you, too, on days when you find it difficult to remember why you're working so hard, or running so fast, or feeling so deeply. All of us forget on occasion and all of us require reminders. It's called being human.

Readers will find no claims of truth herein. The following essays reflect a few interpretations of one woman's life journey. Hence, the only truth they may convey is rather suspect since it's all mine. (And startlingly so in some places. Italicized sections reflect journal entries or personal poetry from similar time periods.) Having been blessed to facilitate so many workshops, retreats and seminars over the years I know this much: that people, no matter how successful or how defeated, yearn for one thing--to know that their life matters and that they have left a garden in some corner of the landscape called life.

Consider this book one flower in mine. I hope it inspires you to grow your own.

Cynthia Barlow, May 2006

A Starting Point: Birthing Love

> "We are all born for love.
> It is the principle of existence and its only end."
> —Benjamin Disraeli

THE LARGE BLACK-RIMMED CLASSROOM CLOCK hangs on the wall across from my hospital bed. It is suspended at eye-level in the middle of the wall directly across from me. I stare at it. It is all I can do; stare at it and watch the seconds tick by in measured doses, like an intravenous drip. It is both excruciating and reassuring in its metronome marking of the passage of time. I think back to my school days and the countless exams where similar clocks – round, bold, plain and all-powerful – sat in judgment of my progress or lack thereof. As it does now.

It is August 12, 1981. I am lying in a bed in a birthing room in a hospital in Baltimore, Maryland. It is my due date and I am, in fact, about to give birth to my first child, a highly unusual overlap of expectation and reality as several nurses remind me. Having been awakened at 7:20 that morning with the breaking of my water, I had had ample time to arrive at the hospital in a relaxed fashion, going so far as to paint my fingernails. This turned out to be an entirely fruitless endeavor as the nurse promptly removed all traces of the beautiful red enamel upon my arrival. A precaution, she said.

It was not until I had called my doctor, checked into the hospital and had the prerequisite enema that the contractions began in earnest. As is my pattern with pain, either physical or emotional, I felt nauseous and vomited several times, ridding myself of the protein milkshake I had carefully concocted and with which I had intended to fortify myself for the impending physical challenge.

So much for preparation.

I had prepared myself in other ways, too. My husband and I had dutifully attended childbirth classes. We learned about the proper ways to hold, bathe and diaper a newborn practicing on dolls. I remember feeling a bit arrogant; I was the eldest of six children after all, and felt quite prepared, thank you, to hold, bathe and diaper a newborn.

We had purchased all the necessary items with which to care for the wee one: crib, changing table, rocking chair, brightly colored decorative items such as a clown lamp, hanging mobile, pictures for the walls. There was an ample supply of disposable diapers, burping cloths to toss over the shoulder after feedings, baby powder, wet-wipes and the obligatory (in those days) rectal thermometer.

I had had a wonderful time choosing a color scheme with wallpaper and boarder print to match. I had taken much time in the selection process and very little with application, being a proficient painter and paperhanger. The year before I had papered the family room while watching the finals of the U.S. Open Tennis Tournament – a five-hour slugfest between John

McEnroe and Jimmy Connors – and had completed the room and cleaned up before they had left the court.

The nursery was ready. It was cheerful and pretty. The bureau was stocked with an assortment of newborn undershirts and stretchy, one piece snap-up sleepers and, of course, many "dress up" outfits of a unisex nature, gifts from friends and family members. They were ready to receive this child, the first grand child on my side of the family, and I was ready to care for it. When asked if I had a preference ("boy or girl?"), I always responded with a non-committal and socially acceptable "as long as it's healthy," but secretly I wanted a boy.

So here I am, six hours after arriving and securing a birthing room, a fairly new concept (in those days) and a welcome alternative to the sterile, antiseptic delivery rooms. I had had a picture perfect pregnancy – no stretch marks, cramping, or varicose veins – and had remained healthy and active thoughout the nine months. I ate well and carefully, measuring my protein intake and attempting to ingest 100 grams (a difficult task) on a daily basis. I had eaten fresh, leafy, green roughage. I had never been constipated. I felt vital, healthy and eminently prepared to give birth. Barring an unforeseen emergency, I would do so in this lovely, floral papered room, eliminating any need to remind myself, visually, that I was actually involved in a medical procedure – a mystery, a wonder, a natural event, to be sure ("Chinese women just squat in the rice fields, for heavens sake"), but a medical one, nonetheless.

And I could have remained in my state of medical denial were it not for the clock, the damn clock.

It is 5:26 PM. My doctor, a wonderful, warm, genuinely caring young man with a new practice, examines me.

"You're about 5 cm dilated. Shouldn't be too much longer" and he pats my knee as he rises from the end of my bed.

I suspect he's being kind rather than truthful. I have dilated only 2 cm in the past two hours. At this rate I'll be here for hours, anxiously awaiting each new contraction and breathing "through" the pain. I am already tired by the breathing and the pain. I am tired *of* the breathing and the pain. I am tired, period, and find it the most remarkable of experiences that I am actually falling asleep and dreaming between the contractions which are coming every 90 seconds or so.

My belly has been strapped with a monitoring device that registers each contraction on a separate machine standing by the bed on my right. Much like an adding machine tape it spews forth a paper chronicle of my afternoon endeavor. The varying bell curves indicate the severity of the contractions; some slow and gentle slopes, some spiked mountains followed by deep valleys.

I try to visualize what is happening inside my body. The crisscross muscles of the uterus are contracting in two directions simultaneously; they tighten across and then down. They are pushing the baby lower into the birth canal. I think the visualizations might diminish the pain. They don't.

My husband sits on a chair to my left, leaning forward and dutifully holding my hand. Through our pre-natal classes, he has prepared for his role as my coach. He is to instruct, encourage and assist me with my breathing. Indeed, he is to breathe with me but he is tired, too, and shortly after the doctor arrives he takes a break himself, checking with me first. He's going to have a quick cigarette, he says. He'll be right back.

As a point of pride, it being the 80's and all, I have decided to give birth naturally. That means drug-free. It is supposed to enhance my awareness and leave the baby healthier and more alert. My sister-in-law has given birth naturally as have many of my friends. If they can do it, I think, so can I. What they've never told me, in the midst of many conversations about their respective experiences ("Oh, it's a beautiful, bonding experience, so much more rewarding than being numbed") is that it is also more painful, *much* more painful. Natural may be beautiful. It may be wonderful. It is also more difficult to endure. But my husband and I have made the decision to have a natural childbirth and I don't want to disappoint him, so I wait until he leaves before asking my doctor for something for the pain. Not an epidural, which numbs completely from the waist down and requires a large needle to be inserted into the spine, but something – *anything* – to ease the increasingly sharp and debilitating pain which permeates my entire body.

He pulls the sheet down over my uplifted knees and a small smile crosses his face. "OK. I have another patient I need to check on. I'll be back shortly with something to take the edge off the pain." He is gentle. He also favors natural childbirth, but I feel no disappointment or condescension in his acquiescence to my request.

I am alone in the room now; alone with my child-to-be, alone with my thoughts, my pain, the monitor and the clock.

I stare at the clock. It blares the time as surely as any trumpeter: 5:37. I see the seconds go by and wait for the next contraction. They are quite severe now. I had thought the pain was bad ten minutes prior when I asked for medication. They are worse now – much worse. I feel I am being torn apart. There is some sort of wild beast inside my belly clawing its way out. I know I am to breathe with the pain, through the pain. A contraction begins and wrests me from my exhausted slumber. I try to breathe in short, shallow bursts but the pain is too intense and I find myself moaning; a sort of primal wail beginning from a place so deep inside me that when it erupts from my mouth I am surprised. Who made that sound? Where did it come from? I am fighting the pain, which only makes it worse, and I want to scream.

The clock on the wall screams instead – 5:48. No husband. No doctor. Where are they? Don't they know I am dying in here, alone and frightened? Something has gone wrong. The pain is too much to bear. I am not strong enough, not prepared enough and for the first time I am frightened; frightened by the pain, by being alone, by the sounds coming unbidden from my mouth and by the clock – the merciless clock laughing at me and daring me to try and alter its control of my situation. I want to give up. I want to go home. I want the pain to stop. I do not think I want this child.

The time between contractions is shortening. Barely thirty seconds have passed since the last one and now another begins. Like waves crashing on the shore during a storm they are fierce and unrelenting. No amount of wishing them away helps to diminish the pressing tide. I am drowning in the waves. I cannot catch my breath. I feel I am being tossed about like an insignificant piece of flotsam.

The clock yanks me from the wreckage. 5:55. Where is my doctor? Where is my husband? I cannot stand the pain any longer. I begin to cry. Not intentionally, it's just that tears have appeared at the corners of my eyes and are trickling down my cheeks. I feel defeated by the waves, the storm, the small beast inside me. I feel defeated by nature.

My husband returns. I point to the monitor in a feeble attempt to convey the severity of the contractions and the accompanying pain. The peaks and valleys show little variance to the display of the previous hour, yet I still try to impress upon him that though it doesn't show on paper there is *much* more pain now than when he left a half hour ago. For some reason this is terribly important to me. I keep pointing to the monitor and crying and trying to speak, to make him understand I'm not making it up, that the pain is real. I don't want him to lose confidence in me. But I have lost all confidence in myself.

He has eaten a tuna fish sandwich and smoked a cigarette. I can smell the pungent odors of both on his breath as he leans forward to reassure and comfort me. My stomach turns in response. I want to throw up again. I can tell he is confused, uncertain of what to do to comfort me in my distress. I don't care. I am uncertain, too. All I want is for this whole natural process to end.

6:02 PM and another contraction. I roll my head from side to side as the power of the wave swells. I don't want to do this. I squeeze my husband's hand. He reminds me to breathe. I try. I want to go away. I want him to go away. I want this pain to go away. The contraction crests, begins to diminish, and then the strangest thing happens; my gut contracts and I feel like pushing. It is called the bearing down reflex. I have been told of this birthing impulse. I have read about it. I have prepared myself, after all, for this natural experience. But nature has defeated me and nothing I have read or heard has prepared me for the intensity, the utmost necessity of this *need* to push impulse. It is indicative of the end of transition, that period of time when the cervix dilates to 10 cm and the child inside has room enough to crawl out. In my pain I have forgotten all this.

6:04 PM and Keith returns to my room. "Hi, sorry I took awhile. Had a quick delivery. Let's see how you're doing." My knees are up and he's between them examining me as I tell him, "I think I have to push."

"Hold on till I check you out."

He doesn't understand. I can't wait. I want to convey to him the intensity of the past half-hour, my fear, my pain, my sense of abandonment. I want him to know what I've been experiencing. All I can manage to do is to reiterate weakly, "I have to push."

Keith's head pops up from his spot at the end of my bed. He is smiling. There is understanding in his eyes. Maybe he *does* know. Maybe he has seen this before. Maybe I'm not dying. Maybe this *is* natural.

"Well, well. You've dilated 5 cm while I was gone. Good for you. You're through transition. You can push on the next contraction."

The next contraction? No. Now. I have to push *now*. It goes far beyond I have to push. It exceeds I *need* to push. It is even well past I *must* push. I CAN'T NOT PUSH!

My belly tightens and Keith says, "OK, Cindy, here we go. Wait…wait…OK. Take a deep breath, sit up, and push…now!"

I follow his instructions. My husband puts an arm around my back and holds me forward as I clutch my knees and bear down. Guttural sounds escape my lips. I am aware of them though unaware that I am making them. The pushing is a relief. It is something I can do. For the first time I feel participatory and actively involved in the birthing of this child.

I have forgotten the pain. I have forgotten my fears. I have forgotten the tuna fish. I have even forgotten the clock. There is a purpose to my pushing. There is a purpose to the pain. And I am up to it. My confidence returns and I can breathe again. The pain is still present and all pervasive with each ensuing contraction, but it is different somehow now that I'm assisting the beast in its exit from the darkness into the light.

"The head is cresting," Keith says, and my husband leaves my side to join him at the foot of the bed.

"Honey look! This is so cool! You can see the head."

I don't want to see the head. I want to get it out of me. I'm tearing apart. I am on purpose now. I am a guide not a tourist and I have no time nor interest in viewing the historical sites.

"One more push now, Cindy." Keith is intent on the beast, his hands between my legs. "One more push for the shoulders – it may hurt a bit more – one more push with the next contraction. You can do it. Take a big breath – and push!"

You do it, I think. I can't – I won't. I'm tired. I want to quit. Let someone else finish. I want to go to sleep. I want to go home, to my own bed, and die. But the contraction comes anyway, and I push, and it hurts and the shoulders pop out and the beast is released, and my son, Michael, is born into the light.

Keith smiles, a genuine smile of acknowledgement and accomplishment. My husband is ecstatic. He is crying and kissing me. I am happy, too. But I am more relieved. The pain has ended, come to a stop on a dime.

Keith lays Michael on my newly flattened tummy. He is not crying. He is not a beast. He is small, and pink, and perfect, and beautiful. I inspect his tiny hands and fingers. I look at his toes: ten of each. His eyes are closed and his face is peaceful. In an instant I fall in love – hopelessly, completely, and eternally in love.

And then he pees on my stomach.

And the clock smiles down at me as it softly whispers "6:28."

˷

Is anyone really prepared to give birth to or to parent a child? Is anyone ever really prepared for any endeavor in life? Is anyone prepared for life? Or love? We can read. We can study and practice. We can talk to experts, listen to tapes, or watch videos. We can pray and hope and beg and complain and weep. We can wait forever to gain the necessary expertise before launching any new venture or we can jump in, get wet and learn some more.

Life offers a series of lessons for our continued schooling long after we have left the algebra books and number two lead pencils behind. The longer I live the more grateful I become for the generosity and persistence of those lessons. Some have hurt beyond my belief in my capacity to bear them. Some have contained so much joy and wonder as to cause my heart to feel that it would burst in response. Some are protracted over a long period of time; most are momentary and elusive, like a child trying to open his hands to glimpse the captured firefly and still contain it. Some have been shouted at me like an angry parent. Others have seemed as straightforward and logical as a college professor's lecture. A line comes to mind I have often used in my classes; if we don't learn our lessons when they gently tap us on the shoulder, we will learn them when they whack us up side the head with a two-by-four.

Nowadays, when I hear the whispers, when I feel the tapping, I choose to listen, at least most of the time, even when I do not want to do so. I have felt the two-by-four more times than I care to remember. The voice of my teacher is too well known, too respected for me to ignore. I hear it as I am demanded to face my own past. I hear it in a phone call from the troubled friend who calls at a most inconvenient time; in the request for directions from a stranger when I'm running late to an appointment; in the resistance from a guarded program participant. I hear the voice of love whisper in my heart and it is incumbent upon me to respond.

I can't not listen anymore.

Lullaby Lament

Tuesday, April 28, 1998

I thought the passage of time would diminish the pain. I thought being physically removed from my children would become easier. But the days have stretched into weeks and the weeks into months now, twenty to be precise, and the pain is still this living, breathing thing inside me. Perhaps that is indicative of some restoration of health. I remember a time when to acknowledge the loss, the loss I created in order to follow my soul's call to a new life in a new city with a new husband, was more than I could face.

Now I am no longer the primary care-giver to two boys. I am an off-site mother. I have carved out a new life for myself, one independent of my former marriage. Remarried and relocated, no one in my new city knows me as the ex-wife of a CEO. They know and respect me as who I am in their presence, by my words and deeds, not who I used to be by virtue of association and marriage, the image of a happy wife I cultivated out of necessity for my survival.

My children have adjusted well after a time of transition. They have, appropriately so, adopted their father as their lamppost and guide. He wanted them, he was willing to raise them full-time after my years of doing so after the divorce and he is doing a fine job of directing them into manhood. But where does that leave me? I used to be their all: their cook, maid, driver and cheerleader. I provided *comfort, advice, admonitions and hugs. Mine was the warm bed offered after a nightmare, the voice that sang them to sleep, mine the smile that greeted them upon waking. What now, when those things which are so very dependent on proximity are impossible to give?*

Andrew's favorite bed-time song was Peter Paul and Mary's "Leaving on a Jet Plane." How many hundreds of times did I sing that song? So many times that, like a practiced dance team, I would tip-toe from his room on the last refrain simultaneously with his slippage into the measured breathing of sleep. What would I give to be able to sing him to sleep, just one more time, without waiting to escape the duty of another nighttime routine; "I'm leaving on a jet plane, don't know when I'll be back again, oh babe, I hate to go..." I missed much with my unawareness of the fleeting nature of those precious nights.

I made a conscious decision to entrust those boys to their father. I relinquished my duties as an on-site mother. At the time the emotional bank account had run dry and I needed to replenish it in order to live and grow. I followed my heart. I followed what I believe to be my calling. I became a well-trained facilitator, a seasoned program leader helping people look at, deal with and heal from their own pain. They write me letters of thanks. They say I have been an inspiration to them. They tell me they will never forget me, that I've made a difference in their lives.

And yet here I sit, tears clouding my eyes such that it is difficult to see the keyboard, wondering if I sacrificed my children for those people. They were just twelve and fifteen when I moved to Toronto. Now, at not quite fourteen and seventeen, they tower above me and the nights of singing them to sleep have long passed. "Now the time has come to leave you. One more time, let me kiss you, hold me close and I'll be on my way. Dream about the days to come, when I won't have to leave again, about the time I won't have to say, I'm leaving on a jet plane, don't know when I'll be back again..."

Dear God,

I am struggling today. I miss my children. I am weepy and feeling sorry for myself. I seem to have forgotten why it was so important to follow your voice. I wonder about the message itself, though deep inside I believe you called me here. Help me to remember. Give me faith to face a summer that will be lacking in as much time with my boys as I had thought I would have. They are growing up and have their own lives. Help me to identify and define my place in them. And help me forgive myself, dear Source of All, for exchanging nights of songs with my children for nights of tears with adults who never experienced a lullaby in their youth. I trust I made the right decision.

Help me to believe it.

On Giving it Your Best Shot

> "My mother drew a distinction between achievement and success. She said that achievement is the knowledge that you have studied and worked hard and done the best that is in you. Success is being praised by others, and that's nice too, but not as important or satisfying. Always aim for achievement."
> —Helen Hayes

I SPENT SOME TIME WITH my sons last week over the US Thanksgiving holiday. On this trip I talked with my eldest son, Michael, concerning his next step in life. He is eighteen years old now and a senior busy exploring his options for college. This can be a daunting task even when you know what you want and an even more overwhelming experience when you're not entirely clear and you're also afraid.

Afraid?! Why, he can't wait to be free of daily parental supervision. He's looking at schools near mountains and can't wait to ski. He wants to continue playing lacrosse and soccer. A social creature, he wants to meet people, he wants...a lot of things. But mostly Michael wants to know he's good enough, smart enough and quick enough to succeed at a new level. Hey, me, too. And isn't that the case for most of us?

So we talked a bit about that while fending off the swarm of holiday shoppers at a local mall. Slightly resistant to the topic initially, ("Ah, Mom, I'm sick of talking about this.") he eventually blurted out, "*I wish someone would just tell me where I should go!*" His frustration was evident. He longed for an easy out, a quick answer. But clarity is not an easy thing to glean sometimes.

Driving home we continued to discuss his various options and feelings. It wasn't long before I came to understand that my son fears two things: He fears choosing a school where he can get good grades fairly easily, but risks the burden of untapped potential and a life-long regret of "getting by"; and he fears choosing a school which may over tax him, thereby cementing a self-image that says I'm not good enough no matter how hard I try.

I see this with clients – fear of failure *and* fear of success. Most adults have the same intrinsic, paradoxical fear of not being good enough while also not living up to their potential. Measuring themselves against a yardstick of perfection, they fall short, feel guilty and continually notch down their own approval rating. At the same time, they begin to resent the elusive standard for happiness, which is seen as "out there" and controlled by someone else (their boss, spouse, parents, etc.).

I told my son at the conclusion of our conversation, "At the end of your college experience, you will be the only one who knows whether you gave it your best shot, whether you got by or really invested yourself. If you can look back and say to yourself, 'good for me', then it doesn't matter what your grades are, nor what your father and I think. In the end, you're the one who'll live with the memories of those four years of your life. What would you like them to be?"

Not a bad question to consider as we turn the page on another year, a decade, a century, and enter a new and exciting time. What memories have you created thus far? Have you set your sights on success and sacrificed the daily achievements of life? Do you concern yourself more with what others say and less with what you believe? What memories would you like to have four years from now?

It's never too late to go to back to school.

Christmas Truths

"We make ourselves real by telling the truth.
Man can hardly forget that he needs to know the truth...
but he can forget how badly he also needs to tell the truth."
—Thomas Merton

MY HUSBAND AND I TRAVELED to three different cities visiting various family members this Christmas season. We opened presents, shared delicious meals and enjoyed each other's company. The greatest gift, though, turned out to be honest self-expression.

The first stop was my father-in-law's new home in Brockville. My husband's family was estranged for many years and this was the first time in eighteen years that my father-in-law had his two children together on Christmas day. It was a very emotional time during which this man, still hurting from the results of his choices through the years, broke down and wept – really wept – with both of his grown children holding him as the weight of those lost years began to wash away.

The next day my husband, Timothy, and I drove to Baltimore to spend a few days at my brother's home. My mother was there and I had the opportunity to spend several hours in quiet conversation with her in a darkened room with only the lights of the Christmas tree to illumine each other. Like many mothers and daughters our relationship has had its "learning opportunities." In addition, being the eldest of her six children, I helped teach her how to parent as my eldest son has educated me: the price of the first born.

On this evening, our last together, we spoke of our feelings, our fears and our love. My mother was gracious and allowed me to tell my truth. It could not have been easy for her. And this time I cried as I felt heard, really heard, for perhaps the first time in my life.

Back in Toronto my husband and I had a few friends in for a New Year's Eve dinner and I listened to a young woman, engaged to be married this summer, talk about her feelings and fears and her love for both her mother and her fiancé. Her mother refuses to accept her only daughter's choice of a husband. The result is confusion, anger and a lot of guilt and resentment. This daughter knows her truth but has been too frightened to speak it yet.

I am reminded that the greatest gift we can give another person, especially someone we love, is the gift of authenticity — who we are, what is important to us, our hopes and fears — and that those things can only be known if we communicate them. There is something so real in the willingness to speak our truth in love as to leave little room for disapproval. The power of expressing our real self offsets the fear of personal exposure. It is in our very authenticity that we meet each other as human beings. It is a courageous act. In fact, telling the truth is the supreme act of courage and the crux of becoming real.

January first of the new millennium has come and gone along with all its hype. We are left, once again, with the person staring back at us from the mirror. Give the gift of truth this year — to yourself and then to those you love.

It is the best road to becoming real.

The Greatest Gift

> "We are all teachers; and what we teach is what we learn, and so we teach it over and over again until we learn."
> —Course in Miracles

LEADING A RECENT RETREAT I was privileged to witness the sacred space created by people joined in a journey of emotional exploration and spiritual discovery. I had a blast, doing what I love and sharing it with others.

My younger son was on my mind this class. Andrew is fifteen and a half and is one of the blessed young people in the world. Bright, gregarious and charming, he is still growing into his six foot, 190 pound frame. He is fortunate to have found his passion at an early age. As a sophomore with a four handicap, he is focused and future oriented. Golf is his current *raison d'etre*.

He was due to visit me in Toronto this past weekend (which he did) and I was busy confirming details with his father with whom both my teenagers have lived since my re-marriage and move to Canada three years ago. This has been a very workable situation and he has been supportive of the boys visiting each month. I do, however, still miss them and can sometimes smack myself with pangs of guilt in order to assuage those pangs of pain.

I had one of those guilt-trips during this retreat. I brought out the list I keep in my head of all my parental mistakes, both real and imagined, and hurt myself for a few minutes. Emotionally bloodied, I let it go, (*again*) knowing that I made the best choices I knew how to make at the time and that based on results, they had been just fine.

I finished the class on Thursday, Feb. 17, 2000. The next day I got a call from a friend, Cricket, who lives in Baltimore along with my sons. She has known my children since before they were born. She called this day, she said, to relate the following story.

Seems she had decided to learn how to play golf. An active woman – physically and spiritually – she also has limited means and knows the price of private lessons. So she's sitting in church last Sunday...

"And I turn around and who's sitting there but Rob and the boys! And I said – Rew! Golf! Hey, how would you like to give me some lessons?"

I could hear the delight in her voice. She continued. "And I told him, 'Now you figure out a fair price and call me with the details and we'll work this out, if you're interested.' He said he was, and he called and we had our first lesson yesterday! In my own backyard! It was wonderful. I learned a lot."

I was thrilled by her story and grateful to hear it, especially since I had been beating myself up so very recently for the lack of my daily presence in Andrew's life. *Others will step in as needed*, I thought, *to guide and support my son as he travels through life.* My heart practically bursting, I thanked her for reminding me of a basic truth. Truly, I said, we are all connected.

"That's not the end," she continued. "After we had finished, we walk over to the house and Andrew clears his throat and tells me I've got some natural ability. He says..."

"'Crick, I wasn't really sure how this would go, I mean, us knowing each other and all, and, well, I was kind of nervous about this and, (his voice picked up and got bright and fast paced) well, what I mean is, this was fun! You're good! I can see us going out on the course and getting a game in. There's a lot I can teach you! I think this will work out.'"

Tears sprang to my eyes. This woman had given Andrew the greatest gift anyone can give another person; an opportunity to share something they value. She was teaching Andrew the joy of teaching. I was wrong about "knowing his passion and following it" being all Andrew needed to know in life. Knowing and following are only two of the prongs of the tripod of one's passion and purpose. The third is sharing it with others – *teaching* it. We are all teachers no matter where we go or what we do, we teach those around us.

What would you like to teach today?

Hard Choices and Heart Scars

> "I have discovered that people are not really afraid of dying; they're afraid of not ever having lived, not ever having considered their life's higher purpose, and not ever having stepped into that purpose and at least tried to make a difference in this world."
> —Joseph Jaworski

ALMOST FIVE YEARS AGO I was faced with a choice. The company for which I worked at the time was closing their Baltimore office; I could continue to fly back and forth to Toronto doing the work I loved, give it up altogether, or consider moving to Toronto. I chose the latter. It was a difficult time and my ex-husband and I spent many months in the presence of a therapist, with our two sons, intentionally creating an agreement that would work for all of us. (At that time, I did not know that I would remarry a Canadian.)

But people change, and children grow up, and sometimes the best of intentions can cause scars.

My youngest son, Andrew, twelve years old at the time, was a bubbling mass of rage: he threw things, he cried, he put holes in the walls of his bedroom. Marcel Proust said, "We are not healed of our suffering until we experience it to the full." Andrew fully experienced the pain of the day to day loss of his mother.

Michael was "fine" with it all. He was fifteen, very cool and unwilling (or unable) to express his sadness. As I said goodbye to him outside his father's home August 26, 1996, tears streaming down my face, he hugged me and said, "It's no big deal, Mom. It's not like I'll never see you again." Michael had yet to release his pain. I, on the other hand, sobbed for most of the eight hours it took me to drive to Canada. I thought I had "experienced it to the full."

Apparently I was mistaken. Last Thursday, my husband and I drove to Baltimore in order to spend Easter break with my sons. While we enjoyed the time together, I found myself blind-sided by two things: my eldest son's residual anger – and my own.

Now almost nineteen and about to graduate from high school, Mike broke his curfew Friday night. Not by much but he lied and the sense of betrayal that bubbled up inside me caught me off balance and triggered the events to follow. Frightened of the potential repercussions Michael said some hurtful things in anger, evidence of his buried pain. He has had a difficult year and had come close to opting out of attending college and even of playing lacrosse, his passion and the sport for which he has been offered a partial scholarship the following year.

On Saturday I realized that Easter fell on the twenty-third of April. That was the day I had first been married twenty-three years ago. I am forty-six years old. Somehow, the preciseness of that mathematical relationship and its culmination on such a symbolic day as Easter caused me to recognize (rather abruptly and with no small surprise) that I had been running scared of my ex-husband for half of my life. I had been apologizing, albeit unconsciously, to my ex-husband and my children ever since moving north for a choice no "good" mother would ever make. While I love my work, my husband and my new life, I was still attempting to earn my sons' forgiveness and my ex-husband's approval.

I was sickened by it. I was outraged. And I felt it – *fully* – for the first time; all the pain, all the anger and all the grief I felt stemming from choosing my own fulfillment over my children's. I wailed and I cried; like a wounded animal gnawing its way out of the trap, I sobbed the sobs of freedom. I wrote a vitriolic letter and burned it and prayed that there might be some relief, some glimmer of new life sprouting – *oh, God please!* – from the bloody stump on which I now limped.

The next day, Easter morning, having opted out of a formal church service, we nonetheless observed the day. Gathered around a small table we each named our greatest achievement of the past year, our biggest regret and our biggest hope or dream for the next year. We wrote down the regrets on little pieces of paper and burned them in a metal pot. We said good-bye to the perceived mistakes of the past (an ongoing process) and hello to the hopes for the future.

I made a choice almost five years ago, a hard choice; I chose living over dying and I chose to follow the little voice inside that whispered too loudly to be ignored. When we ignore that little voice we deny who we really are. We wonder why we start feeling as though there's something missing in our lives, that happiness eludes us or that we've fallen short of the mark, that we haven't really made a difference. It is easier to stay the course than to look life in the eye and make a choice to live.

That which causes scarring is generally painful even if it is of our own choosing. But scar tissue is stronger than its predecessor and as any athlete knows, it promotes improved performance in future endeavors. Heart scars can be our excuse for dying – or our reason for living.

I choose to live.

An Easter Follow-up

Last month's column was as raw in its exposure as any newsletter I have ever sent. I sat on it for several days and came very close to not sending it, considering opting instead for something safer, something less revealing.

The response was staggering. From corporate presidents to housewives, the story of the Easter visit with my children apparently struck a chord. So many of you have taken the time to contact me – to comment, to share your own stories, to thank me – I felt a postscript to that particular installment was warranted.

> "The greatest thing in the world is for a man to know how to be himself."
> —Montaigne

THE VERY NEXT WEEKEND AFTER my Easter breakthrough, at Michael's request, I again drove to Baltimore in order to see him play in the biggest lacrosse game of his senior season. His team was playing their arch-rivals, a much bigger school with a stronger team, and they were playing in a huge University stadium on a Saturday afternoon. Michael didn't expect to win the game. He just hoped his team wouldn't lose by too much.

Mike's team won the opening face-off and the center passed him the ball. A midfielder, he can run like the wind. The excitement was palpable; both sides of the stadium filled with very noisy teenagers and some passionate parents. I had a good view of the field – at the mid-field line and up about ten rows. Mike was on the close side of the field and moving down the sideline.

He had been very nervous before the game, practicing shooting at the goal in the backyard – and consistently missing. It was his stick, he shouted, it wasn't shooting straight. He didn't feel well. He was tight. He was tired. He had a lot of reasons why he could justify a less than perfect performance that day. I made the mistake of pointing that out before he stomped out of the house with a teammate in order to dress and ride the bus to the game. My last words, uttered to his back as he walked to the car with slumped shoulders, were "Just give it your best shot, Mike. Forget about winning – just play up to your own standards."

He got into the car without looking at me, giving no indication he had heard my words.

I know my son. He's a carbon copy of my self (God's joke) and I can read his mind from a dozen paces face to face – or from ten rows up while he's moving. After receiving that first pass of the game, in the few seconds it took him to assess the field and his teammates' positions, (everyone was covered) my son made a decision to take the ball to the goal. He gave it his best shot that day by taking a chance that might not have been a popular choice that early in the game. This was not a fast break situation. "If it is to be, it's up to me!" he declared silently in the roar of the crowd. Mike turned his head toward the goal, accelerated, faked his defender to the right and then rolled left, beat his man and took the shot.

And scored! His teammates swarmed him. The first goal of the game whether they won or lost was a moral victory. Our side of the field went crazy and the bigger, stronger side went mute. It was a magical moment. And I was there to witness it. I lived it. I felt it to the core of my very being. It was worth seventeen hours on the road in two days to be present for the first minute of that game. I saw my first-born step into himself and into his purpose, as he defines it at this point in his life, and give the game, the team and himself his best shot.

They ended up losing the game, but Michael walked off the field a winner. As I left, a newspaper reporter was interviewing him on the sidelines, the leader of the losing team with a smile on his face.

I drove back to Toronto a couple of hours later, pulling in at 6:00 am Sunday morning, April 31, 2000, with a smile on my face. And I sent the newsletter out that night as it was written. It was my best shot.

∽

Duc de La Rouchefoucauld said, "We are so accustomed to wearing a disguise before others that eventually we are unable to recognize ourselves." Perhaps in my emotional nakedness last month some of you caught a glimpse of a self long forgotten – or long disguised – and recognized the shadowy wisp of authenticity. The **real** you that wonders if it is worthy of peeking out from behind its various masks for fear of being noticed, ignored, or – worse still – denied.

It may be the greatest thing in the world to be your self, but it is certainly not the easiest. Being real demands your time, your attention, your entire *being*, a willingness to tell the truth and a truckload of courage. It is not for the faint of heart. But it is the heart that benefits from the effort expended in the pursuit of self-truth. It becomes stronger and, paradoxically, more sensitive.

I had a call from a gentleman who is registered to participate in *The Trust Program* this summer. He was touched, he said, by my open sharing but he just wanted to make sure he had gotten the message. What was the point of the May newsletter? Having worked with him before and aware of his analytic need to put into a structured format that which often defies logical explanation, I answered in kind, as best I could, logically, attempting to summarize the various intertwining points from a writer's perspective.

Words I had recently stumbled across crept into my head as I spoke. "A mind all logic is like a knife all blade. It makes the hand bleed that uses it." I smiled to myself and ended the explanation. "The main point of that newsletter was the same as any of my newsletters – to make you think. Just to make you think."

It is also my intention to help you feel...*yourself*.

Perhaps the chord struck by the last month's newsletter was simply the echo of your own heartstrings being plucked in self-recognition.

If so, what a symphony was sounded!

Essential Freedoms

"We look forward to a world founded upon four essential human freedoms. The first is freedom of speech and expression...the second is freedom of every person to worship God in his own way...the third is freedom from want...the fourth is freedom from fear"
—Franklin Delano Roosevelt

TODAY CANADIANS CELEBRATE THEIR BIRTH as a nation. In three days the United States will do so as well. As a US citizen who has chosen to live in Canada I want to acknowledge and celebrate both independence days. This year I'm celebrating something else; the freedom from fear of remembering.

Fifteen years ago when my sons were still just toddlers, long before the dark shadows of mid-life awakenings had begun to lengthen, the Easter Bunny brought a present to our home. Our first dog had died the previous year and my eldest son, Michael, had taken it particularly hard. Mike had dictated a letter of request to the Easter Bunny a few days prior to Easter. My husband and I agreed that the family was ready for a new addition to our family and so our second dog had been chosen from the breeder the night before. We decided on a female chocolate Labrador Retriever.

After discovering her on Easter morning, eight weeks old and blinking awake in the midst of a new reality from the safety of the box of rags in the laundry room where she had slept the first night in her new home, Michael declared her name to be Megan. Puzzled at the time, I asked him why Megan? He knew no one named Megan. He didn't know why he picked it, he said. Her name was simply Megan. End of discussion.

Megan grew to be an extraordinarily strong and determined swimmer, capable of crashing through four-foot waves breaking on the beach in pursuit of whatever had been thrown for her. We trained her well (though she became a terrible beggar, a result of my indulgences) and she would heel without a leash standing still by my side until released. Rather suspicious of strangers — I always had to have a good grip on her when someone came to the house — she served as a wonderful watchdog. My husband being gone quite a bit as he built his business, I felt completely protected by this dog. No one came near my house that I didn't know about it.

Over the years, Megan became as much a part of the family as the children. The mutual devotion became a deep-rooted reality, a given. Her needs were taken into consideration when making plans, we included her in family photos and her presence was often required for a small boy to be able to fall asleep at night. Though she would not tolerate being "cuddled" she would dutifully wait until the child's breathing was slow and steady before scratching softly at the closed door, a signal she had completed her duties and wanted her own bed now.

Her bed was in our bedroom underneath a highboy bureau. Perhaps thirty inches off the ground and well delineated by the four tall Queen Anne legs which supported it, the bureau was her sacred space. The routine was always the same: she'd come in when it was apparent that I was headed to bed, flop down in her space, put her head between her paws and watch me until I'd finished my nightly routine. When I had gotten into bed she'd scurry over to my side, sit down, lean her body into the side of the bed and plop her chin up onto the top. *You may love me now* her eyes would twinkle.

So I would love her, stroking her deep brown fur which became sun-streaked in the summer, telling her what a good girl she was, such a *good* dog, the *best* dog I had ever had, *such* a good dog. And her eyes would close slightly and she'd soak up the tone of my voice like a sponge. When she had reached complete absorption, she'd go back to her spot, curl up and go to sleep.

When Megan was seven the dark shadows dimmed the light in our home for a few years. She became my pain-sponge, absorbing more than her fair share of tears. Four years ago Megan made the journey north with me when I moved to Toronto. After marrying, a key component of our decision to live near Lake Ontario was the proximity of the water and Megan's love of it.

By then she was starting to slow down but she could still make it to the water and back. In her last year of life she had lost the use of her hind legs and most of her sight. Watching her age and caring for her until the end was like watching a piece of my self die; I was thirty-one years old when she entered my life, I was forty-five when she left. She represented my youth and all that goes with it, the illusion of immortality, invincibility, and an ignorance of some of life's immutable lessons.

Last June it became apparent that Megan's quality of life had deteriorated to such a point that I decided to have her put to sleep. It was the first time in my life I've made a conscious decision to end a dear one's life. I was choosing to say goodbye to Megan and to a huge chunk of myself which was, at one time, the entire chunk of me by which I judged myself worthy; how I looked, what I accomplished, what others thought of me.

A year ago today, Timothy and I drove Megan to the vet's office and said good-bye. My sons were present. Her eyes were completely clouded, her muzzle white, her body large and lumpy. The day she died she was beautiful and dignified and magnificent. I saw only her essence that day and her unshakable trust in and devotion to me.

Today I am remembering all that Megan taught me: the price of freedom, the inherent glory in living true to oneself, the gift in grief, the nature of compassion. She helped me to release my rusted emotional shackles and I helped to shed her physical ones.

Today I am allowing myself to review all the wonderful memories I have of Megan, without regret or sadness. I am choosing to believe that wherever her essence now exists she is running full tilt into waves her head high, her eyes sharp and locked on her target, full of herself and living free.

Today I am celebrating that I not only decided to do the same but that I live in a country where I am free to attempt it.

In Memory of Megan

"As a well-spent day brings happy sleep,
so life well used brings happy death."
—Leonardo De Vinci

I wrote this piece July 2, 1999, the day after Megan died. It was a cathartic thing, a way of remembering in the midst of letting go, and of honoring her life in the midst of her death. If you have ever lost a loved one may I suggest that you read it in your bed with a box of tissues handy, and then go to sleep remembering the good times.

∽

I STOOD AT THE KITCHEN counter, eyes unfocussed, looking toward but not through the large picture window that filled the wall in the dining room over looking the river. Waiting for the coffee to brew I was aware of the sucking and spewing, the rhythm a familiar and comforting respite on this day. This morning my brain seemed to have seized, like an engine run dry of oil, refusing to move. I stared ahead, seeing nothing but a rolodex of images from the past flipping behind my eyes. Pictures from the past, the past which included Megan.

The knowledge of this day's arrival had scurried across my

consciousness many times, swept away before the knowing could leave dirty footprints on the floor of my heart. I had had much practice in the art of brushing away, covering over, boxing up, filing away hurts in obscure categories.

The coffee maker stopped its spitting, the absence of the audible cadence drawing my attention back to the present. I reached for a mug hanging on the wall behind the stove and placed it beside the coffeepot. My arm felt heavy; lifting it required effort. I added cream and sugar, tested the blend with a sip and then wandered past the kitchen butcher-block island into the main room of the cottage.

My father had purchased the cabin over forty years ago as a summer cottage, an island retreat from the unrelenting spiritual and emotional tending and round the clock access demanded of a parish priest. Having graduated Columbia University with a degree in industrial engineering the same summer he felt called into the ministry, my father had carefully planned each summer's expansion project and looked forward to the chance to exercise the side of him that loved logic, balance and symmetry. He would quite literally "put his house in order" annually. This was before the demands of his chosen profession had taken their toll; before his youth and sleek good looks, his intelligence and vibrancy, had been leached from him and deposited in the bottom of a bourbon bottle.

The original cabin had been a small box of a thing, perhaps 20 feet by 20 feet and as his family grew he had added rooms and a second floor to accommodate what finally became a brood of six children. He had declared that it was *not* cheaper by the half-dozen and had finally announced the end of breeding season with a vasectomy. He said that he and my mother were in the 1%

of the population for whom various forms of birth control just didn't work--the wink with which he said it an indication of the pride he took in his virility. He liked his large family.

I paused at the intersection of the cabin's traffic patterns--the open kitchen behind me, the living room in front--the dining room to my left, and allowed myself another memory. Perched on stilts extending out over the water, the dining room had once been a porch. The placement of the room provided a panoramic one hundred and eighty degree view of the river through giant windows on three walls; the sunsets through the western window could convince visitors of the existence of a divine Michelangelo.

I had painted the beamed ceiling myself. White ceiling, brown beams. Dad said I had a steady hand and good eye for straight lines and detail work. I always did the window sashes when windows came up on the repair rotation. Every few years or so there was something major to do. Repair the porch, replace the septic or rebuild the dock. My brother had titled the family book in which we continued to record necessary information for whoever opened or closed the cottage, "The journal of never-ending maintenance endured in the name of vacation."

I love this place, its perfect Tropicana-tan stained pine walls, the floor a similar toffee color patchwork quilt of 36" wood squares. Andrew had taken his first steps on this floor as the entire family spent a week on their hands and knees, sanding and shellacking the newly enclosed dining area. At night with a fire burning in the copper hooded fireplace the entire place was bathed in a creamy warmness I have yet to experience anywhere else. Like a loving grandmother, buxom and tender, the room gently holds visitors close and soothes any hurt. I love this place with a passion bestowed only on my family. The magnificent St. Lawrence River, or at least our little piece of it – the loon warbling on the water, the pine trees whispering in the wind, silence surrounding all – is the touchstone of permanence in my life.

When I was little I thought the trees could talk. My favorite thing of all was when it rained at night. I would lie in my bed cocooned in my quilt, listening to the syncopated rain drops tap dancing on the roof that my father had built, feeling protected and secure and completely safe from all "things that go bump in the night." I still love the sound of the rain, but have come to realize that things that go bump in the night are more often met in broad daylight.

I would do this thing in daylight. I would put Megan to rest, finally. Megan, who had guarded me, absorbed my tears, helped raise my sons. Young men they were now, Michael almost eighteen and Andrew three years younger. They lived with their father now. Then, they had lived with both their parents. Then, they were only four and one and the shadows had not yet fallen on their sense of safety.

I drifted into the main room and sat down in the padded rocking chair, my father's chair. I had listened to him read aloud from this chair, year after year, until I had heard C. S. Lewis' Narnia chronicles, all seven of them, three times through. My father's voice was a thing of beauty, as were his hands though he rather fancied his calves, a result of his years on the Columbia swim team.

When reading aloud or performing the liturgy, he spoke from a deep place, a place that some stage actors and preachers find, the place at the base of one's spine where the voice hurls itself from captivity, like a fisherman casting a net, and captures the listener. It is the storyteller's place where magic can occur. My father could take sentences and carefully dip them into warm honey, coating them with the seduction of secret meaning. He changed pitch for different characters. He used his eyes to convey significance whenever Aslan, the heroic lion and main character, spoke. He became Edmund and the White Witch. His body never competed with the magic of his voice. It was his voice that breathed life into those characters, into his sermons, his counseling sessions and his youth group meetings. His voice breathed life into words. He would hold court in the summer evenings, mesmerizing those children old enough to be caught in the net, snaring them so that they would plead for more at the end of a chapter. Sometimes he would give in but more often than not we would be told to "wait until tomorrow night," the promise of another adventure dripping from his voice. Being the eldest, I had more conscious memories of those early years, the years of his splendor.

His voice was his dowry to me. I had inherited a female version of it and painted "word-pictures blind people can see." At least, that's the way a former student described it. My next younger sister had followed my father into the ministry. She, too, could hold an audience spellbound. My mother had been an actress, taught speech and held a master's degree in directing. And *her* father had acted in silent movies, eventually running a theater group in Duluth, Minnesota. Performing is a part of my heritage.

Much of my heritage is visible in this summer cottage. It is far more than a two-weeks-a-year place. Each year from mid-June to early September my siblings and I had spent the entire summer on this island, within these walls. Each year, as we pulled away from the dock to return to "the real world," my father would turn around and say "Good-bye tiny house," and we would all say "Good-bye tiny house" and I would cry, as the house became even smaller in the distance. I had a hard time with good byes. *I should have known then*, I thought as I rocked in the chair. *I should have known.*

It was a good thing I didn't know then what I knew now, that my heart would be broken, as well as my children's, that my husband would leave, that I would leave my sons, my home town, my country. *Thank goodness I couldn't see the future.*

I rose from the chair and poured myself another cup of coffee. *It's time*, I thought and walked toward the phone. Flipping through my mother's small dog-eared address book of summer friends, workmen, and service people I found the number I needed and dialed. An answering machine announced that the Doctor's office was not yet open for the day. I left my name and number, made my request and then returned to the chair. I had planned to do something productive but couldn't for the life of me think of anything more important than to sit in that chair.

Megan lay outside on the porch. She could no longer get down to the dock for her meals and was unable to get into or out of the water. She had had to be rescued from the water twice, the rocks being too slippery for her aged hind legs to find firm footing. She had stopped trying after the second rescue. Now she just slept most of the day or whimpered when she woke and found herself alone. Mostly blind and deaf, she was increasingly anxious and a new, higher pitched tremor of fear had crept into her plaintive barking.

Ah Meggie, my Meggie. You were once such a strong swimmer. I gazed lovingly at my cherished pet and in spite of myself tears sprang to my eyes. *Another good-bye.* I caught myself and wiped my eyes. Memories flooded my mind, memories of Megan, memories of my sons. *They were so young then.* I rarely allowed myself to go back there anymore. But as I continued to watch Megan sleep, I made a conscious choice to return and replay it one more time, one last time.

It was an Easter morning when she first arrived…

Dear Easter Bunny,

Please can you get me a doggie? I want a tan one, that's really nice, that doesn't bite. I want a puppy that will love me and we'll train her to be good, and go for walks with us. Please bring a leash with her. Thank you very much.

Love, Michael

Dear Michael,

Since you left me such a nice letter and your mommy and daddy said you are a big boy now and can take good care of a dog, I have left a surprise Easter present for you in the laundry room. Take good care of her.

Love, the Easter Bunny

P.S. I couldn't find a tan one. I hope brown is OK.

Megan was curled up in a box of rags under the workbench in the laundry room. The pile of softness had been an inviting escape from the loneliness of separation from her mother and siblings the night before. She peered out over the edge of the hacked down cardboard box, blinking herself awake as the family of four entered with whispers.

"Where do think she is?" I asked opening the door. Michael, alert and eager to see his little boy wish-come-true, squeezed around me to be the first to find out. His eyes, always the first to see the little things of life, the stuff which made it a place of wonder and worry, darted about the room and landed on the dark brown mound of fur with frightened eyes looking back at his own, and stopped his forward movement.

"Over there." His voice hushed as he knelt down on the cold linoleum floor and looked back over his shoulder. "Mommy, look! It's a puppy!"

Andrew, only eighteen months old and still wearing diapers, scurried toward his brother. He was big-bottomed in a light blue sleeper with rubberized soles and his heavy-footed shuffling interrupted the silence of the discovery. Not quite understanding the significance of the moment, he was nonetheless as caught up in the excitement of the new family arrival as were his parents.

Standing behind the boys I smiled up at my then husband, leaned into his solid frame and squeezed his waist. I remember that morning as a particularly happy one: my husband, my sons, contentedly living the good life of the American dream. I had the house in the right neighborhood, I had produced an "heir and a spare," as my father had joked when Andrew was born three years after Michael. I had a station wagon and now a dog. There were Easter baskets, a jelly bean hunt and chocolate bunnies. We smiled, we touched and we reveled in the completeness of it.

We also wondered about the name. Michael had more than chosen it. He had declared it within minutes of meeting his new dog.

"What do you think, Michael? Should we keep her?" Rob moved to pick up the ball of fuzz. "She's kind of pretty. What'd you think?"

Michael jumped up. "I want to hold her," he said, a statement of ownership, not a request. His little brother bobbed up and down as his knees waggled back and forth in a physical expulsion of internal energy. Andrew was already exhibiting a characteristic that would prove to be permanent, a physical child to Michael's verbal one. "Me hold too, me hold," he repeated as he held out his own little arms.

"No. She's my dog! I get to hold her first." Michael sidestepped into his brother, established his position and reached for the fragile puppy.

"Hold on guys. She's very little, and she doesn't know us, and you need to be gentle. Andrew, Michael gets to hold her first. You can hold the puppy after Mike. OK?"

Rob placed the pup in Michael's arms. "What's her name, Daddy?"

"I don't know, son. I don't think she has a name yet." Rob glanced at me and I took over.

"Sweetie, she came here for you. I think *you* should name her, if you want to." Michael interrupted me. He had been quietly holding his new best friend in his four-year-old arms.

"Megan," he said.

I returned my husband's glance with slightly raised eyebrows. "Uh, well, honey, you don't have to name her right this minute. You can think about it if you want. There's no rush; a name's an important thing." To my knowledge, Michael had never heard the name before, there were no children named Megan in his pre-school class, no one with that name in our lives, no TV characters. Where had he come up with that name?

Michael looked up at me.

"Her name's Megan, Mommy," he said again, firmly and without raising his voice. "Megan," he repeated as he looked down at his newly baptized dog and stroked her tiny back. "She's Megan."

⁓

I remember a conversation Mike and I had before Megan arrived when he was about three years old. We were sitting at an intersection in downtown Baltimore when out of the blue and apropos of nothing he said, "Mommy, I bet you Bucky's up in heaven guarding God's throne."

I laughed and responded, "Well, honey, if there is a God up in heaven and if he does have a throne, I just don't think it needs guarding. At least, I hope it doesn't."

Quick as a wink and with earnest child-like wisdom Michael shot back, "Oh, Mommy. *I* know that and *you* know that," his voice dropped to a whisper, "but *Bucky* doesn't know that!"

This was not the first time Michael had introduced God into a conversation. A year or so earlier we had lost our first dog, Buck, when he was run over by a car in our neighborhood. Mike and I had witnessed the unhappy event and the memory of it lingered. Shortly afterwards the two of us were traveling somewhere in the car when he suddenly asked a question, completely out of left field. "Mommy," this child pondered aloud, "what weapons does the devil use?"

Startled, I can remember exactly where we were on the road at that moment, as I attempted to formulate an answer for this budding theologian who still sat in a safety seat. *Where had this* question come from? Michael was a big fan of a TV show called "He-Man." He-Man had a special sword he would raise toward the sky while proclaiming loudly, "I am the POWER!" I assumed some reference to the devil was in that show at some time.

I sputtered forth a few of the seven deadly sins, as best as I could remember them. "Uh, he uses... ah, greed, and um ..." Lust I thought. *No, let's not open that door...* As I stammered out another deadly sin, Michael interrupted me. My answer was not computing and he was losing patience. "No, Mommy, I mean does he use guns and knives and swords?"

I sighed in relief. *Ah, guns and knives and swords. Of course!* This was his perspective on "bad" power. "Yes honey, the devil uses guns and knives and swords," I responded.

I glanced at Michael in the rearview mirror. He was looking out the window, his ever-present, tattered stuffed animal and best friend, Woofie, tucked under his chin. *What was going on in his head?*

We passed a few moments in silence. Slowly his head turned back toward me. "Well," Michael spoke deliberately, "then what weapons does God use, Mommy?"

Holy smokes! I understood Mike's dilemma. What on earth could possibly beat a sword? In that instant I had no answer. I shot up a little plea. *Help! What do I say to this child?* My mouth opened as if of its own will and out of it fell, "Love, honey. God uses love," and I felt a flood of feeling infuse my body and I knew I had just experienced the truth of a state of being represented by a word – love – that I did not even begin to understand at that time in my life. To this day I credit that moment as the beginning of a journey attempting to understand my own answer to my child.

Megan became a distinct part of that understanding. She taught me much about devotion, compassion, and courage. She demonstrated component pieces in the love puzzle, without words, without confrontation. She loved me unabashedly. She loved my sons dutifully. She loved her life exuberantly.

⁓

I closed my eyes and leaned back into the softness of the antique padded rocking chair in my father's summer cottage. A fire burned in the fireplace, the seasoned wood snapping and popping as it consumed itself. I had turned off all the lights, only the glow of the fire to illumine the room. The river had grown still at dusk, as it often did, but tonight there was a hint of a storm in the distance; the wind was beginning to pick up. I let my head drop backwards against the chair again, this time leaving my eyes open and allowed myself, for the first time, to replay the events of Megan's last day. None of it had been as I had originally planned and it had all unfolded in a perfectly symmetrical pattern that exceeded my own design.

My sons were lodged in the sleeping cabin behind the main cottage with four of their teenage friends. Young men now, they had driven nine hours from Baltimore for a week of sun and fun on Hill Island. Six was a few more than I had wanted to tend at the beginning but Michael had persuaded me with two sentences. "But Mom, these guys might never have the chance to experience such a spiritual place. I want to share it with them." Sold.

There was one footstep on the back porch and the door opened. Michael entered the room. "Hey."

I turned at the simultaneous sounds and smiled. "Hey yourself."

Michael paused, his hand still on the doorknob, "You want to be alone?"

"No. I'm glad for the company. Come on in." My gaze returned to the fire as Mike walked to the couch and lowered himself in one movement into a horizontal position, feet plopped onto the bench in front of him and extended toward the fireplace.

"You OK?"

"Yeah."

We sat in the silence of the firelight. I had long since learned that his physical presence indicated a desire to be with me, to connect, to feel a part of, to remember. Words were a secondary aspect to our relationship. He would speak if and when he chose. His hair was blonde, a result of a recent weekend at the beach with his girlfriend. I had remarked that with the humidity and his natural curl he looked like Harpo Marx. "Who?" he had asked.

Mike shifted his legs, a signal. "She was a good dog." It was both a statement and an invitation. He glanced at me.

"Yes." I turned and met his eyes. "She was a good dog."

Mike's head returned to a frontal position.

"You have everything you need out there? You guys comfortable?" In spite of myself, I wanted more words.

"Yeah."

"There're extra blankets in the closets if you need them."

"We're OK, Mom."

We passed a few moments in quiet. Then Mike initiated interaction.

"I really loved her." He continued to stare at the fire.

The statement required no response and so we sat in companionable silence. The wind had increased. Rain was surely close on its heels. The sound of the waves lapping on the shore was quite audible and insistent. *Ah, Meggie, I miss you so much.*

⁓

She must have known. Michael and Timothy had put her into the car that morning, her hind legs no longer able to support her weight. I had made the appointment on Monday, three days prior. The boys and I were to leave for the island on Thursday and it just made sense to leave Megan in Toronto. Nearly blind and deaf, her hind legs were a withered joke of her previous strength and she had become incontinent. She spent most of each day sleeping. When awake she whimpered. It was the thought of her being so frightened all the time that demanded my decision. I suddenly realized that it would be cruel and selfish to ask Megan to make another trip to die on an island simply because her mistress had envisioned some sort of storybook ending. I always desired storybook endings. I decided to let go of writing this one.

When I left the house to join Timothy in the car, Michael was bending over Megan in the back seat saying goodbye. He had placed a dog biscuit in the space between her paws as she had always taken comfort in a morning "cookie". After closing the car door, Mike turned and hugged me, holding me, allowing himself to be held, and we cried. The embrace ended and I walked around to the passenger front seat. Mike sat down on the front steps and put his face in his hands. His eyes were red and he cried without apology.

In the end, Megan's exit took perhaps twenty seconds, an

economical exchange rate for so rich a life. With Megan in the back seat, Timothy and I drove the five blocks to the veterinarian's office in silence. The ride was too short, too quiet. It being a national holiday the hours of opening had been moved to 10:00 AM. We were the first appointment of the day so the waiting room was empty, much to my relief.

The receptionist was on the phone, apparently with someone who was asking a lot of questions. As I stood and waited the scene outside was visible through a window behind the receptionist's desk that overlooked the parking lot. Timothy was trying to get Megan out of the car and it was obvious she did not want to move. Two workmen in blue overalls entered the waiting room behind me from a door leading to the examination offices. Conversing congenially they quieted as they passed, a quick glance at my face summarizing the situation. Through my haze and even in my numbed state, I noticed and appreciated the gesture of respect. They exited the office into the parking lot and became a part of the scene through the window across from me.

Timothy had hold of Megan's paws, his coaxing having failed to budge her, and was pulling her slowly toward the open driver's side door. This door faced the workman's truck so that they were unable to access their passenger side. They stood and watched, not impatiently, as Megan dropped to the ground and immediately scurried as best she could around the front of the car. Timothy followed. "This way girl. We're going this way."

Meagan turned and scuttled around the front of workman's truck. It was then that I noticed the sign on the back of it. It was the cremation company. The two men gently began to participate in the chase, stepping aside and forming a sort of wall between Megan and the parking lot beyond. As Megan veered towards the building again, I went to the door, opened it and called to her. It was at that point, I later thought to myself, that Megan had acquiesced. Something of the fight left her – it was in her eyes – and she entered the office directly.

The receptionist ended the call and within minutes all the administrative details were handled. Megan sniffed the perimeters of the room displaying none of her usual anxiety upon once again finding herself at the vet. Normally, she would pant profusely, finding a spot on the floor from which she would refuse to move. This time however, she seemed to have a kind of curious resignation, much like that of a college student arriving first semester to find their room already occupied by an assigned roommate.

The doctor came out and asked if we wanted to be present. We did. We followed him through the labyrinth of inner doors and examination rooms to one far in the back. Megan followed right behind. A green plaid blanket had been neatly folded and placed on top of the examination table. I thought it quite soothing, a strangely pretty and considerate thing to have a warm blanket underneath rather than the usual cold metal of the tabletop. Later I would remember the plaid of it and find it an interesting image to have been so indelibly burnt upon my brain.

Another man in a white coat was there, a young man with kind eyes and a soft voice. "We'll need to lift her up." And we did, in one swift, sweet last movement. Her head dropped between her front paws extended out in front of her and stayed there.

The doctor had an electric clipper in his hand. "Hold her head. We'll need to shave her leg a bit for the shot." Four short, methodical swipes later and he held a needle in his hand. I looked up. "How long will it take?" The words seemed to stick in my throat. Everything around me seemed to be operating in fast-forward while I moved at half-speed. It felt surreal, like awakening from a dream still caught in another reality.

"Not long. Perhaps thirty seconds or so." He held the needle aloft, pointing straight up. "Are you ready?"

I looked back to Megan, straight into her clouded eyes and nodded once. I was aware of the doctor beside me, my husband behind me – I heard him sniffle quietly, but I saw only Megan. Spoke only to her.

"It's OK Megan. What a good dog you are." I stroked her head and back. "You're such a *good* dog, Meggie." The doctor inserted the needle and began to push the plunger. "I love you, Meggie. You're *so* good." I bent my knees so that I was directly at Megan's eye level. "You've been the *best* dog I ever had." The needle was removed. The doctor raised his forearm and to look at his watch. "It's Ok – It's Ok. You can go now Meggie. I love you Meggie." Timothy had stepped forward to put an arm on my shoulder as much for himself as me. "We love you Meggie," he whispered through his tears. "We love you Meggie," I echoed. "You're *such* a good dog."

The watch was replaced by a stethoscope and placed on Megan's chest. "She's gone," he said quietly. But I had already known that. I knew the moment life had left Meggie's body. Her head had gone limp and her open eyes had deadened several seconds earlier and I had known, known in an instant that the fur I was stroking, so soft and thick, so full of the illusion of life, no longer protected the spirit within.

I straightened somewhat and draped myself over the mound of brownness before me and gave full reign to the emotions held in for Megan's benefit. I grabbed huge fistfuls of fur and clenched them as if to prevent her from leaving. *No, I screamed to myself. No! Come back. This was too fast. I'm not ready. I'm not ready to let you go. I want one more day. Just one more day. Oh, Meggie, Meggie. I miss you already.*

The two doctors had departed the room discreetly leaving Timothy and me alone. We stroked Megan and reiterated our love for her and then turned to each other for solace. Eventually we left the room without looking back. Holding hands, the drive home was silent as well. Again, too short a ride for so heavy a sadness.

The boys had packed up and were vacuuming the house. Michael was on the phone. He looked up and said, "It's Dad." Finishing, he handed the phone to me.

"Hi," I said quietly as I walked upstairs to my office. I wanted no witnesses to this moment. "I was going to call you."

"I just thought you might want some support. Tough, huh?" His voice was the voice of a friend, lacking any traces of our angry past, replaced now by the memories Megan evoked. The good times, the young times.

"Yeah, it was tough." I reached my desk, melted into my chair. "Oh, Robbie, it was so hard...and it happened so fast, I wanted to say *stop*. I missed it. As soon as it was over I wanted to scream 'come back!'"

I cried aloud, sniffling into the phone, knowing that this expression of me, my sadness – with which he had always had great difficulty – was invited today. A hand offered in the darkness of my heartache. Out of earshot now I spilled forth my feelings of the event, as a way of including him, but also a way of connecting to, of clinging to, the hand extended by the man who had shared our past and our youth. We talked awhile, reminisced and even laughed a few times.

It was not until an hour later, ready to pull out for the three-hour drive to the cottage, my eyes puffy and sore, that I had reason to open the back door of the car to place a last minute item in the space Megan had so recently occupied.

The cookie Mike had placed between Megan's paws lay untouched on the seat.

⌒

The wind was whispering loudly now, demanding to be heard. The large oak tree just behind the main house had joined the pines in announcing the rain's imminent arrival.

Mike removed himself from the couch, ready to return to his friends. He approached me and leaned down to kiss me goodnight. "Love you, Mom." His eyes met mine only inches above my face. I smiled the smile only mothers seem to own, a visual declaration of unconditional love and my eyes misted over. "I love you more," I said.

"Love you more than more." Remembering our old childhood litany, Mike smiled too, the smile of tolerance sons reserve for their mothers. Straightening himself, he was at the back door in three steps, pausing as his hand met the doorknob. Turning, he looked back at me. There was a gleam in his eyes, a surprise ending.

"Know what, Mom?"

"No. What Mike?" My voice mimicked his eyes, a straight man for the punch line.

But the gleam faded into something softer, his eyes seeing beyond me, beyond the fire, the wind, and the river. His voice grew softer, too.

"I bet 'cha Meggie's up there guarding God's throne."

My throat tightened as I responded. "I bet you're right, Mike. I bet you're right."

"Night, Mom."

"Goodnight Mike."

I turned back to the fire and gave into my feelings. *Ah, Meggie, Meggie, my heart aches with missing you.* The wind whispered its last and the rain began, a gentle thing this time, arriving quietly but with authority. The drops danced on the roof overhead. I closed my eyes and listened. So many voices lived in this place, my father, my siblings, my children, my God, and now Megan – some of them gone, but not forgotten, never forgotten. The beauty of their voices lingered in this place.

Images flashed: Megan retrieving sticks from the water; my father, healthy and happy swinging a hammer; Michael as a ten year old swinging on rope out over the water and dropping *ker plunk*. My heart brimming with the memories of happy times, I wept tears of gratitude and joy for those I had loved and lost. I believe they have not left, just moved on to a different place, a better place, a place of peace and possibility. The wind returned causing the rain to change cadence from consistent to intermittent sweeping across the roof. I leaned my head back and gazed at the ceiling as my tears subsided.

The wind was speaking and the rain demanded that I listen.

"Do not weep. You have loved me well. I am not gone, nor do I sleep, for I am now whole, and young, and I can run and see and hear again. The sounds of life surround me and I am wild and free and full of possibilities. There is

no anger, nor fear, nor restriction of any kind. I am alive. I live in your heart, in your mind, in your children. I am your past, your present, and your future. I am the voice in the wind, the flame in the fire, the rain on the roof.

I am patience, I am love, I am loyalty and devotion. I am kindness and consideration. I am persistence and reliability. I am the best part of yourself and those parts yet to be developed. Listen to me. Hear me. Know that you are loved beyond measure, beyond time, beyond space. I am a part of you forever for I have loved you unconditionally. Go now, and do likewise for I am with you. I am here. Always and forever.

I am always.

I am forever.

I Am."

Trust Your Swing

"The longest journey in the world is the one we travel
from our head to our heart."
—Cynthia Barlow

ANDREW TURNED SIXTEEN ON JULY 6th. He's my golfer, has a two handicap now and placed second in the Maryland State Junior Championship qualifier last week. He missed the cut for the Men's State Open by a stroke, the result of teeing off from the wrong box and incurring a two-stroke penalty. He knows the rules but hadn't checked out the course before the match. It's the kind of thing that only experience teaches.

Most of Andrew's life at the moment revolves around golf and getting his driver's license. We spent at lot of time in the car together this trip. He did the driving. I did the watching: him, the road, traffic and all the variables thirty years of driving have taught me. The stuff you can't learn from a book or a lecture or a movie.

I would caution him now and again, offering what I saw as bits of wisdom. I think he saw it as something else. His most common response (other than "woops") was "I know." He would sometimes follow that up with a direct quote from his driving manual, no doubt an answer to a recent question on a test.

Experience teaches us how to perform under pressure. Andrew's head knows a lot; his body has a slower response time. He knows the information and only time and experience will teach him *how* and *when* to apply it at a moment's notice. He's very good and still, there were a couple of moments where Andrew's lack of experience revealed itself and I found myself responding involuntarily with sharp intakes of air and firm clutching of the armrest as my right foot attempted to stop the car by stamping down on the passenger side floor.

And I teach people how to trust!

It is a constant thing, this trusting business, learning how and when, where and with whom and how much and if it's deserved or not. In the end, it all comes down to a leap of faith. My son is about to have legal access to a vehicle in which, according to statistics, he stands a good chance of being killed. It's up to me to trust in him as much as he trusts himself.

There is a commercial I like: Vijay Singh, winner of this year's Masters, is shown addressing the ball about to tee off. Various golf admonitions appear alternately superimposed over his still form at various angles in different fonts and sizes, one on top of another. As he turns his shoulders and raises his club behind him, at least twenty reminders – "Head down," "Keep your eye on the ball," "Check feet alignment," – morph one into the other indicating all the thoughts flowing through his brain as he takes his club back. The camera follows his progress in slow motion.

At the top of his back swing, he pauses. All the words disappear to be replaced a half beat later by one clear, bold statement directly across the top of the screen. Another half beat and the Masters' master unwinds his body in regular motion to smack the ball straight down the fairway. The screen goes black as we hear the gallery cheering. A final phrase is emblazoned across the dark surface screaming the way. A victory cry of faith across the abyss between information and experience, the directive is a warrior's words of wisdom: "Trust your swing."

It is said that maturing can be likened to attending University: a freshman *knows* he knows it all; a sophomore *thinks* he knows it all; a junior thinks he *doesn't* know it all; and a senior *knows* he doesn't know it all. I trust that Andrew is on his way to becoming a senior.

And that the universe will be kind to him as he makes that journey.

Personal Branding

> "The symbol is not a sign that veils
> something everybody knows.
> On the contrary, it represents an attempt to elucidate, by
> means of an analogy, something that still belongs entirely to
> the domain of the unknown or something that is yet to be."
> —Carl Jung

RECENTLY I SAW THE MOVIE, *The Patriot*. I hadn't really wanted to go, it being three hours long and besides, I knew who ended up winning the war. But it was Mel Gibson, after all, and an opportunity to see my mother and sister-in-law. So we went to a big screen, got a personal pizza and munched our way through a recreation of the birth of the United States of America.

In one of the final scenes the British are advancing. The voluntary militia, led by our hero Mr. Gibson, is a ragged and rowdy group of untrained soldiers. Faced with an endless onslaught of wave after wave of redcoats they begin to retreat. The newly designed symbol of their efforts – an American flag, its red and white stripes stained with the blood of the men who had carried it, its blue square with a superimposed circle of stars tattered – falls to the ground. Realizing his men have forgotten the reason behind their efforts, the why of their pain, our hero picks up the flag and runs toward the British shouting "Hold the line men!" I doubt I am giving anything away by saying his men follow and it all goes well.

The point is this: I had a visceral reaction to that scene. In the minute it took to witness it, I recognized the yearning of the human heart to belong, to understand, to fight for and defend the values behind and in the symbol of freedom as represented by that particular flag. It is my flag. I was born under it, I was raised with its mythology and legends and I understand in a glance the common culture contained in its image. I experience a similar feeling when I gaze at pictures of people I know and love. Their face is their *brand*.

Of the fifty or so people in the audience that day, I'd bet I might have been the only American citizen present. And probably the only one to cry as hard in response to something so deep that it caused me to ache.

Today is Wednesday, August 30, 2000. Yesterday I spent some time with two friends. One of them called me this morning with some news. Our friend's daughter had been killed in a car accident late last night and our meeting, scheduled for today was canceled.

There's a lot of talk about branding these days. "Create your personal brand!" as though it is something mysterious outside us, waiting to be given life with our creation of it. Each soul is an individual brand. It does not need to be created; indeed it can *not* be created. Rather it can only be uncovered, revealed, discovered, found inside. It can only be acknowledged, developed, given full expression and finally lived.

It is in our *living* that we create our brand. And it is that imagery – our life – that lends significance to the symbol we create to represent what cannot be named. It can only be felt. When I look at the picture of my son that sits on my desk I am reminded that I imbue that picture with meaning because I understand who he is and know what he represents. In that picture I see his soul. I see his essence. I see his "brand."

Today I am aching for my friend as he begins to enter into a new reality, an irrevocable one that now no longer contains his daughter on a physical plane; her indelible spirit, her untapped potential, her gifts to the world, to her family and to her father. I had just recently met her. It was a lovely, warm evening. Only a few years older than my son, I connected with this young woman all too briefly. I felt touched by her openness, sincerity, and gentle spirit.

Farewell Erica. Your brand lives on.

Worry Shadows

"Worry often gives a small thing a big shadow."
—Swedish proverb

A FRIEND OF MINE HAS two children. After many years of focusing most of her attention on her eldest perceived "problems," my friend has developed a habit of worrying. While most parents do this there is a difference between *concern* for the well being of one's child and *worrying* about that child. My friend had worried her way into a pattern that was now pushing her children away from her.

As she continued to talk, my friend expressed concern for her younger daughter, now a junior in high school. She was seeing the same patterns of behaviour and attitude once expressed by her elder sister. "Guess I have a new one to worry about," she said. *No, you just have a teenager,* I thought to myself.

However unconscious we may be of them, our fears will eventually become self-fulfilling prophesies. I think my friend's attitude will eventually create in her younger child's life some crisis because that's what she fears, another "problem" to be dealt with. She thinks her concern is justified. Perhaps it is. Or perhaps her personal "worry screen" is making it real. This attitude is very attractive to her for several reasons.

"Worry affects the circulation, the glands, the whole nervous system, and profoundly affects heart action," says Charles Mayo, M.D. In fact, worrying creates nothing but stress that negatively affects our spiritual, emotional, and physical health. So then why do we worry? Several reasons come to mind.

First, we have been conditioned to do so. Most of us have plenty of role models in our life who have set a wonderful example on how to worry well. I've met champion worriers. They have ribbons of excellence attained in worrying, emotional trophies of their angst. We call these people martyrs. They are not fun to be around. They often have plenty of physical ailments to go along with their emotional traumas. They suggest that their worrying is a sign of their love and devotion. It is not. It is a sign of their unwillingness to "let go and let live." If we have been raised by someone like that we can begin to think that not worrying is an indication of not caring. This is not the case. Letting go of worrying is not about complacency. On the contrary, it promotes more effective choices.

Second, we think that worrying will accomplish something, that to do so actually moves us toward a solution. It does not. It simply maintains the illusion that we are actually *doing* something to solve the problem about which we are worrying. In fact, all we're doing is spinning our wheels. Worrying is like pressing harder on the accelerator in order to dislodge a car from the mud when what we need to do is go get a board to provide traction.

Third, worrying is easier than not worrying. It requires less "consciousness." It's such an automatic response that it requires less effort than choosing a different one. Choosing to look for solutions requires a conscious effort, which is often uncomfortable, and human beings tend to avoid discomfort. As Robert Frost said, "The reason that worrying kills more people than work is that more people worry than work."

My friend has one other reason to hang onto her worrying. Once she stops, what will her life be about? From whence will come her sense of purpose? Once her younger daughter comes of age, where will my friend direct her focus? What else will bring meaning to her life when her children have moved on?

I posed these questions to her, gently, as she listened on the other end of the phone. It is not an easy thing to change one's filters on the camera of life. I suspect my friend will struggle for a bit with her answers. But that is how we learn best sometimes, by struggling to find our own answers.

Kind of like teenagers.

The Value of Pondering

"No one can walk backward into the future."
—Joseph Hergesheimer

I'VE BEEN PONDERING THE WORD acceptance lately. It being a new year, I looked at the one past and the one upcoming and did my rather usual and perfunctory comparison attempting, once again, to set some personal and professional goals. New Year's resolutions. Which set me to thinking about the word "resolve" – to re-solve. *To re-solve what? My life? Last year? This year? Things don't need solving.* Which led me, ultimately, back to the notion of respect.

Actually, "acceptance" is the current tangent of my two year pondering of the word "respect" and what it really means to respect someone or thing. *What does it feel like? How does it show up in speech, in body movement, in choices, in relationships?* I tend to ponder things a long time, especially when I drive long distances and I drive a lot.

I know it's been two years examining this respect thing because I remember the moment it sprang into my brain. Driving south to Baltimore I had exited I 90 at Batavia, New York, to cut down Route 63 on my way to I 390 South. I paid the .95 toll, turned south along little Batavia's tree-lined street, and saw a sign stating the designated speed limit: 30 MPH.

I play this game on long, well traveled routes to well known destinations. Marking off times and distances while noting various landmarks, I check the time and start measuring. *OK, 45 minutes to the split, then an hour, unless there's construction..."* always attempting to make it to where ever I'm headed in "good time." Speed limits, at least at that time, rather than a case for safety, were a challenge, a gauntlet thrown demanding to be beaten or at least fooled.

On my well-practiced route south Batavia represented the beginning of a back-road stretch where I could "make good time." I'm sure I had noticed this particular speed sign before (and ignored it) but that day, for some unknown reason, I saw it in a different light. I saw myself as a rude guest in their home, carelessly disregarding a request to remove my snow and salt covered boots before entering their newly carpeted living room. I gazed at the sign, now staring back at me as I waited for the light to change. *You are welcome to travel through on your way,* it seemed to say. *While in my home – my town limits – allow me the right to state my own preferences. Please respect my rules.*

When the light changed, I adjusted my speed to accommodate so simple a request. And started thinking ...and thinking... and thinking.

Right now, to get back to the point, I'm peering into the crevice of 'acceptance' and here's what I see:

- That in accepting others **as they are** I respect them and myself. *In modeling respect, I demonstrate love.*
- That it all starts with *me* accepting *them*, and *all* things, AS THEY ARE, not as I would have them be. *Personally, I'd*

rather it was the other way round.
- That choices made from "should," "ought," "need," or "have to," usually taste bitter and often cause heartburn.
- That acceptance means living without an external reference point. *Comparisons are pointless and a waste of time, energy, and intellect.*
- That authority and respect are only sometimes the same thing.
- That no matter which way the kaleidoscope of life turns, it all comes back to love.
- That it's a new year and I could use a new word. *I'm thinking about dignity or honour.*

Pondering is a good thing.
I think I'll make it my New Year's resolution.

The Price of Perfection

"Imperfection is the wound that lets God in."
—Ernest Kunst

PERHAPS TEN YEARS AGO SOMEONE sent me a poem. I don't remember who or when, only that it has occupied a space in my office ever since. I love this little poem and have long since memorized it by constant reading. There was no author attributed and so I thought perhaps it was one of those cyber-space from-the-universe things that simply becomes common domain, but every time I read it I continued to wonder who had originally penned it. It goes like this:

> *"Isn't it strange that princes and kings and clowns that caper in sawdust rings and ordinary folk like you and me are makers of eternity?*
>
> *To each is given a bag of tools, an hour glass and a book of rules and each must build, ere his time has flown, a stumbling block or a stepping stone."*

Fast forward: I have moved three times since then, survived a divorce, remarried, re-formed my life and started a business. The same little poem sits on the shelf behind my desk. Imagine my surprise when I met the author at my (new) mother-in-law's home this year on Christmas day! Nearly blind and well into his eighties, he and his wife were visiting Toronto. He has published many volumes of poetry. He married my husband's mother's husband's sister five years ago. (Read that again slowly) Does that make this remarkable poet my step-uncle-in-law?

There he was at the Christmas table engaged in conversation when suddenly I hear him reciting my little poem. I was speechless. How do you know that poem? I inquired. "I wrote it," he replied, "when I was 12 years old." I wanted to run and shout to the world, I know who wrote this! This little poem – a small thing, but so much more! It was a part of the fabric of my life. Its author had a name. And I now knew it: Glen Moorehouse. There is so much power in putting a name to things. It's like filing them away under "DONE."

Here's the point: I think our wounds are like that. They cast a shadow in our lives. All our imperfections and the "should's" of our lives. All the ways we fall short, don't measure up to some imaginary (and generally impossible) standard of perfection. They all begin to merge and become our "common domain" and eventually, we are hard pressed to name the "author." What caused what, what step or decision or event led to the others in our lives?

I think most people tend to measure themselves against a yardstick of perfection. Even if we understand *intellectually* that it's impossible, *emotionally* we tend to do it anyway. So we compensate for **feeling** "less than" by **doing** "more than." This rat-race mind-set spawns eventual self-loathing as we increasingly define our worthiness by what we *do*, instead of who we *are*.

When we forgive ourselves for being less than perfect, an amazing thing happens: we create space for an experience of the Divine. Those humbling moments when we truly admit our faults can be the most rich, freeing experiences of our lives. God is, has been, and always will be waiting to remind us of our inherent beauty and worth if only we would turn around. When we finally do, we realize the shadow was cast, *not* by an event we perceive as a mistake or another example of how imperfect we are, but rather by our stubborn refusal to acknowledge the divine light of love in which we always and forever stand.

It is in our *being*, not our *doing* that we are most worthy. It is in our wounds and their healing that character is created. It is in our recognition and acceptance of the shackles of shame we have strapped on that we finally glance down at our ankles, only to find we're wearing ruby slippers and have had the ability to "go home" all along. Sometimes it happens when we're not looking for it, after many years of wondering, out of the blue on a Christmas day. And then, rather than a daunting task, the mysterious and sometimes obscure – but always miraculous – process of revelation becomes a cause for celebration, a reason to shout from the rooftops, "*I know its name!*"

You can't turn a stumbling block into a stepping-stone until you know its name.

Spring Cleaning and Sisters

> "The great thing and the hard thing is to stick to things when you have outlived the first interest, and not yet got the second which comes with a sort of mastery."
> —Janet Erskine Stuart

WE GAIN AN HOUR OF daylight today. Spring is sprung and with it comes cleaning.

I'm not much in the way of a house cleaner. Things like windows, baseboards, the tops of pictures frames. While some people actually go searching for dirt (my sister-in-law is a gifted dirt buster) I do not. I tend to putter about, putting things away. I like things to *look* clean and neat, not necessarily be clean and neat. I like to *arrange* rather than organize.

I am, however, more than willing to perform personal, internal clean ups of dusty corners of my emotional basement. I am so committed to emotional and spiritual health that I began a homeopathic sequential healing process many months ago in order to clean out the cellular residue of past emotional and physical traumas. I am convinced that the seeds of most chronic illnesses sprout in the build up of emotional "dirt" left untended too long.

This remedy process, like most undertakings, seemed simple and sensible when I first started it. It is a long-term approach to physical and emotional well-being. Now that I am well into the emotional and physical effects of the cleansing, my original enthusiasm has dimmed somewhat. Working backwards in time from the present, I am currently "cleaning out" the emotional residue of three major losses: my father's death, my ex-husband's marital exit, and my own move to Toronto. Like tackling those final few boxes never unpacked from a previous move, it feels like a lot of work at the moment. I lost my voice two weeks ago, have had clogged sinuses since and generally feel yucky as my body sheds residual, cellular "dirt." I must actively remember *why* I believed this process to be important enough to have started in the first place, in order to sustain my commitment to continuing it.

On top of that, my husband and I have decided to move. This means packing up all our stuff. It also means cleaning – *lots* of cleaning.

We listed the house on Wednesday last week with the first showings to be tomorrow. I attacked the accumulated clutter with great determination: the old stack of magazines under the living room end table; the piles of papers and materials scattered about my office, the old grout in the tub. I picked up, put away and threw out a lot of old stuff. I arranged and lightened. I discovered and vacuumed places I never knew existed. I saw immediate and tangible results. After placing fresh flowers around the house on Thursday I sat back and patted myself on the back. The place looked great.

Except for the basement. That's where those unpacked boxes live. Do I want to carry them as is to the next house? If not, they must be opened and examined. In addition, all the carelessly hidden remnants of Christmas had been casually tossed on top on piles of junk ("*I'll do it later*") creating a real mess. Hmm...what else wasn't I seeing?

I began looking at every room in my house through a buyer's eyes ("What needs to be done to it before I move in") instead of the seller's eyes ("You should have seen it before!") I started in the kitchen and noticed all those little bugs that insist upon crawling into light fixtures to die, creating large collective burial grounds above our heads; and the greasy film coagulating on the tops of the cupboard doors, and the dust on the top of the curtains, and the easily accessible and often used – but highly unaesthetic – kitchen accessories. As I took inventory I realized how much remained to be done in three days. The idea of a new home began to lose some of its luster and my enthusiasm for the entire moving process ground to a halt.

Friday found me wallowing in my own pity party. Physically I felt lousy, emotionally I felt overwhelmed and intellectually I felt frozen: I had not a single inspiration for this month's newsletter. And I missed my sisters. I've got five siblings: three sisters and two brothers. We are a close bunch. When I'm not feeling right with the world they are the people to whom I can go and vent my troubles. (It's in fine print of the birth contract; they must listen.) Due to various reasons, most of them logistical, I've been out of touch with my siblings for over a month. I felt lonely and sad and unable to do anything remotely productive. I longed for the sound of a sisters' voice.

I finally called my homeopath. She said my physical and emotional symptoms were normal healing reactions to the remedies I've been taking under her direction. In fact, the decision to move was probably a related thread. She suggested I watch a sad movie and have a good cry to assist with my body's draining process, but the Raptors were playing and so I watched the basketball game with my husband instead.

The next morning (yesterday, Saturday) with the sinus pain once again acute, I decided a good cry couldn't hurt. Always an over achiever, I saw her sad movie and raised her a tape recording of my father's funeral. Closing my office door I punched play and listened to the eulogy with my family members reading psalms and lessons. I even sang along to a couple of hymns. And I wept steady tears requiring many tissues.

My sister-in-law, the previously mentioned human dirt seeking machine, stopped by shortly afterwards in time to be able to affirm the effectiveness of my morning's endeavor with one glance at my face. My eyes were now tiny red slits and I couldn't "breed true by doze." Dressed (if one can call it that) in my bathrobe, I was in no mood to be sociable. I was in no mood to clean. I was in no mood to be inspirational.

But there she stood, this almost sister, rolling up her sleeves while reaching for the dirt ammunition: buckets, mops, scrub brushes. Her presence wrested me from my sniveling and raised my energy level ("I'm not alone!") We talked, we worked side by side in companionable silence and she shared some of her dirt snaring secrets. The aroma of lemon scented Mr. Clean began to permeate my house. By dinner time the kitchen sparkled, all burial grounds had been moved, the walls gleamed and the basement was cleaned out and neat!

After a hard day something I enjoy is a bubble bath with candles and soft music. Sometimes my sisters have created that experience for me as a way to express affection. Last night, while my husband prepared dinner for the three of us, I went and drew a warm bubble bath for my sister-in-law. I got a clean white terrycloth robe for her to wear afterwards. I lit some candles and put on some soft music, poured a glass of wine and invited her upstairs. As I closed the bathroom door I thought how much I loved her.

I learned a few things yesterday: that the part of any process which requires active assistance versus passive participation is best accomplished in the company of a person who understands the difference; that sisters come in all shapes and sizes and are not necessarily determined by blood relationship; and that one ought never – no matter the intent – to leave a candle burning anywhere. However, if one is going to do it, let it be in the bathroom with its safe ceramic tile.

Today I will find a straight edge razor blade and carefully skim the splattered wax off the wall, the toilet tank and the floor. I'll clean and scrub away all the remains of the once lovely candle that melted down to nothing last night while we ate dinner and watched a movie.

But I'll be smiling while I do it. My sinus pain is gone and I'm breathing through my nose once more.

God Sings For You

God is like a feather bed
In which one sinks to rest a head
Filled with worries and cares
And all the things that scare.
And into that bed, warm and close
We sometimes retreat the most
Forgetting She's there all along
Singing her love in a song.

    If only we'd listen, the song could be heard:
       Like the crackle of campfire
       As it burns ever higher
       With laughter surrounding
       Or in waves pounding
       Against rocks made from time
       Oh! Such rhythm and rhyme
       Or the sound of the breeze
       As it moves through the trees
       In the rain from above

God sings us His love.

If only we'd listen, the song could be seen:
    Like the colors of flowers
    In afternoon hours
    Spent wandering slowly
    In places most holy
    Like meadow and wood
    Under nature's green hood
    Part of the grand master's plan
    All tomorrows it spans
    In all of creation
    God displays Her attention.

If only we'd listen, the song could be smelled:
    Like the fragrance of a newborn
    Or a roasted ear of corn
    Or a lily, leek, or rose
    All for your nose!
    Or a freshly baked cake
    Topped with candles to make
    A celebration of you
    And all that you'd do
    If only you knew
    That God sings for you

If only we'd listen, the song could be tasted:
    Like a meal made with care
    So gentle and fair
    Or a special warm treat
    Fresh from the oven all heat

Or the sweetness of a kiss
When one has long missed
The presence of a special one
And now the waiting's done
If only you knew
That God waits for you

If only we'd listen, the song could be felt:
Like the hug of a mother
Who cares as no other
And soothing the child
So recently riled
Is like the sun shining warm
Protecting you from all harm
And all that has gone before
Is put aside for evermore
With soft textured touch
God loves us this much

Yes, if only we knew
That God's love is true
That He does wait for us
After all the day's rush
To hear the sweet song
For which we so long
The language of love
Sent from above
The sweet song of life
To end all our strife

All our worries and cares

CHICKEN SHI(F)T FOR THE SOUL

All our problems and scares
That we take to our beds -
They live in our heads!
When we open our eyes
To see the blue skies
Or the birds on the wing
Then maybe we'll sing
The song from above
God's lullaby of love.

In the Echoes of Silence

> "No longer talk about the kind of man a good man ought to be, but be such."
> —Marcus Aurelius

MY SONS TOLD ME OF an event that had recently rocked their community; a young athlete of sixteen had secretly videotaped himself having sex with a fourteen-year-old girl without her knowledge and then played the tape for his fellow lacrosse teammates.

The school, home of the top ranked U.S. High School lacrosse team, took the high road by expelling the original offender, suspending the viewing offenders and canceling the lacrosse season thereby potentially jeopardizing the University bound athletes of what surely would have been the national championship team. It is the kind of story that causes rubber-necking in print.

My initial reaction was a pang of sorrow for all those families involved, particularly the young woman. The media have devoured the story, spewing forth their endless versions and explicit details on the national stage to the extent that there is talk of turning this unfortunate event into a movie, an even sadder testimony to a very sad incident.

I was next concerned for the school and the damage to its reputation. Founded over one hundred years ago by St. Paul's

Parish, my father was Rector there for twenty years as I was growing up and my brothers and sisters and I had all graduated from St. Paul's. The school and its deep-rooted lacrosse tradition are a part of my heritage. I remember it fondly. I remember it as a safe place. Perhaps it was simply a safer time.

Apparently the videotape was viewed by teenagers other than just the lacrosse team, Baltimore's private school community being very close knit, and students who had not actually seen it had certainly heard about it long before its existence became known to any adults. My eldest son, Michael, who attended the school until 9th grade, played both soccer and lacrosse in the middle-school with many of the now senior lacrosse players. I have stood on the sidelines with the mothers and fathers of some of those boys. I know these people. These are the people I left behind – by choice.

That's a polite way of saying that the focus of life as I experienced it while moving in and around the people there was one of comparison, gossip and judgments. That's not to say that there weren't also some delightful people. But where one lived, what kind of car one drove, how much money one made and how one looked were too often the measurements for a successful life. Scratch below the surface and there was a mean streak under too many smiles.

My divorce had been public knowledge and certainly my choice to move to Toronto had been ripe fodder for the gossip mill. Upon subsequent returns to the city I had on several occasions experienced being shunned: the quick glance from a former sideline mother in a mall as she turned and walked away pretending not to have seen me; the overt dismissal of my presence by another at a wedding. In neither case did I acknowledge them either, and so the no-man's zone was clearly delineated.

I found that my initial reaction was followed by a too close after-shock. "What goes around comes around," I heard myself say, the previous slights flitting across my memory bank, as though I'm some sort of expert on karmic events. It has caused me to think about my lack of tolerance for these women, my lack of compassion, the very things I had expected from them. I thought about the initial thrill of self-righteousness that played in my heart a brief tune of utter triumph. For a moment I could picture a little mini-me shaking her fist at all those people I want no part of – the ones who had judged me so harshly – followed by a sickening silence in which I was invited to examine my own judgments of them.

Last night I took a bath and found myself musing about one mother in particular, someone I no longer know, as she no longer knows me. I thought about her pain, living with sidelong glances and double-speak. I thought about the questions she and her husband must be asking themselves, as any parent would whose child is thrust into the news in a lurid, life-altering way. I thought about the questions I have asked myself about my own parenting, my own choices and their consequences.

And I thought about all those young men, most of whom – *God, please!* - must have heard the sounding alarm, a call to speak out, an invitation, not just to *man*hood but to *person*hood, to stand up and name what all of them must have known: this is wrong! They will live with the collective scar of a tainted spring season at a formative stage in their lives, but deeper and more damaging are their individual self-inflicted wounds; the scars they will carry for their silence, their lack of response, their choice for group acceptance over personal integrity.

Gandhi said, "Be the change you wish to see in the world." The after-shocks in my own heart to an event so far away compel me to take a closer look at more subtle implications. Tolerance, compassion and forgiveness are attitudes and ways of *being*, not just things one *does* on occasion. It's one thing to *be* polite. It's another to *live* courtesy and respect; it's one thing to *think* something's wrong, it's another to take a stand and *say* so. It's one thing to be aware of one's short comings; it's another to look them square in the eye and name them for what they are.

Let others debate, as the journalists have and still are, the implications of this sorry situation: the lack of parental involvement, the evidence of our moral decay, and the pressures of athletic elitism. Rather than the circumstances themselves I'm going to continue to examine my own responses to it, for therein lay the clues to true and lasting change.

It starts one person at a time.

Fingerprints on the Ceiling

"It does not matter what the outside of a boy or girl looks like, any more than it matters what the outside of a house looks like. It's what goes on inside that counts. The grandest mansion in the country can be a very unhappy home, while the simplest cottage can be the happiest place in the world."
—Margaret Fishback Powers

I SPENT SOME TIME AT my family's summer cottage on an island in the St. Lawrence River over the May holiday weekends. Every summer since I was three years old I've come home to this place. It is a "due north" in the compass of my life, something reliable, known and comfortable beyond description, sort of like a pair of friendly, well-worn jeans. I know every tree and rock, every bump along the path from the dock to the house.

Victoria Day weekend at the end of May we opened it up, dusted cobwebs, made beds, and removed the tokens of affection left behind by grateful winter rodent renters. The opening and closing process has its own inherent rhythm, an order to things and a pacing: dust before sweeping, sweep off shelves before putting staples away, make beds while it's still light. It's a cottage thing; there are certain rituals and traditions, as anyone who has a cottage will tell you.

My Dad built this place, with the questionable assistance of some of his six offspring, room by room, year after year. Splinters were a way of life, carrying pine boards from the dock up to whatever project my father had in store for us that summer. We could all swing a hammer, though with varying degrees of accuracy. Few escaped without at least one blackened thumbnail each season.

One summer my father decided to add a large (by cottage standards) master bed and bath with a sliding glass door opening onto the deck overlooking the water just a few feet away. We all helped. It's the most private bedroom, has a primo view and best of all it has its own small bathroom. When my Mom is not there her room is prime pickings. She wasn't there this trip. I snagged it.

The ceiling above her bed (my father having gone to the great lumberyard in the sky twelve years ago) is now dotted with the aged stains of varying fingerprints, evidence of the many family members through whose hands the wood passed on its final journey. When first placed side by side the individual planks showed none of these remnants of human contact. The passage of time combined with the residue of human skin oils and fresh-cut pine boards has produced an increasing emergence of distinct, darkened imprints. One can distinguish at a glance a child's smaller, paler imprint or an adult's firmer hold. As well, there are several sets over top of one another, blending together, primarily a small child's, indicating several attempts at fitting the tongue in groove on the roof's sloped surface.

Lying in my mother's bed, alone in the silence of wind

and rain overhead, I gaze at the ceiling. Memories of the many summers I have spent here wander across my mind. Traditions, myths, and messages – the once invisible fingerprints of my life made visible by time. I think about the fingerprints on the boards above and the stories they tell. I think about the prints I don't see, not only above me but within me. And I think about the invisible fingerprints left in the lives of my children. They require time to become visible to the eye. But they reside already in the heart and mind.

Last weekend was the Memorial Day holiday so my younger son and his girlfriend drove up from the States, arriving in time for a glorious sunset. I sat on the deck outside my mother's room with its panoramic view of the majestic river and watched my almost seventeen-year-old boy-man-son show his first love something he loves. "Over here's where we swim, you just gotta' watch out for the Zebra mussels. Up there's where we hang out in the sun and play Scrabble. Over here is where we carved a heart in the tree for Uncle Halsey's wedding. There's this huge pike that hangs out by the front dock. We call him Walter. He's here every year, and every year I try to catch him…"

Watching them walk around this special place, I could see the residue of the countless people who have touched my son in his life: his deceased grandfather, his aunts and uncles, his cousins, his father, and me. There are invisible fingerprints all over him. I trust they will continue to evidence themselves in constructive ways as he matures.

Human beings need traditions. We need stories. We long to define and make sense of the invisible imprints still naked to the eye but known to the heart. We attempt to reassure ourselves with proof of what we know instinctually: that in this tapestry we call life, none of us weaves alone – indeed, we weave side by side – and that there is no separate loom per life, only the universal one on which we weave our own small scene in our own small space.

It can be as beautiful and as intricate as fingerprints on a ceiling.

The Day It Rained Cement

SEPTEMBER 11, 2001:

The day began as any other. I flipped on the TV as the coffee brewed and watched a bit of *Good Morning America*, nursing my coffee as I do each morning, the start of another day. Just a simple Tuesday morning, sunny and clear. When the report on a fire at the World Trade Center interrupted the show, I watched with my sister and wondered at the spectacle, never suspecting the ultimate impact of what we were about to witness.

Expecting only to sit a short time until details were forthcoming and wanting to use it productively, I picked up my current project, a crocheted bedspread I was making for my niece for Christmas, a pretty concoction of blues and lavenders and greens. It represents many hours of my time and love. Samantha is only three and a half years old and she might not appreciate it as much now as she will when she is older, but that's OK. I am very close to Samantha and want to give her something that she will value longer than any current passing interest. I want to give her something that will last.

I watched as the horror unfolded, unable to move from the television. I spoke to friends and family who called to give virtual hugs, a verbal testimony to the power of paradigm shifts, a remembrance of things truly important. Watching in disbelief as the second plane crashed into the Trade Center tower, I felt like I was watching a Hollywood movie. The night before – *was that only last night?* – we had watched the highly touted first installment of Tom Hanks' ten part World War II series, "Band of Brothers." Computer generated airborne attack scenes recreated brutal assaults.

Not today. This was real. No computer in the world could generate what the world's eyes witnessed today. Those who died today will not get up again to play another part in another movie on another day. I alternated between dumbstruck numbness and utter grief, a piercing of *something*, some place deeper than any piercing I have known so far in my life.

I was born after Pearl Harbor, but I remember John F. Kennedy's death: a fifth grader, the school closed early and we were all sent home. When Martin Luther King was shot, I remember my father's face as he heard the news and shook his head. Tears came to his eyes. Looting broke out across the city that night and since we lived in the center of downtown Baltimore, he stayed up all night in order to protect his family with a gun in his lap in the front hall of the house.

I remember where I was when George Wallace was shot and crippled and what I was doing when I heard the news of Robert Kennedy's death. But they were far away things, things that wouldn't last.

I will remember this day, too. I am an American. My country

was attacked today. The unknowns of the future loom large in my heart even as it stays anchored to the anguish of all the lost lives in the present. My sense of outrage, grief and horror is disabling. As I type these words I feel exhausted and numb. I want to lash out at someone. Where is my generation's Hitler? There is no convenient face upon which we can pile our collective frustrations. There is no singular nation whose butt we can turn over our knee and firmly spank. It is a collective face, a collective evil, and it flourishes in many places and has many faces.

But let us not lose sight of the enemy's name. Let us not forget the power of naming a thing for what it is. Today's tragedy is merely symptomatic. The disease that spawned this kind of horrendous act of desecration is the result of a world wide illness. It has been spreading for a very long time. Its name is *fear*.

And I sit here crocheting a blanket made from love, *for* love, and wonder how long it can last in a world where the tallest building in the biggest city can be felled to the ground in a matter of moments. Yet it is important to me to continue to believe and so I sit – all day – watching images I will never forget, as they happen, thinking of my family, crocheting a security blanket of love.

The world changed today. The blister burst. It can be the catalyst for healing or infection. Winston Churchill's words keep echoing in my head: This could be "our finest hour." I *must* choose to believe it. Not to do so would be to announce fear's victory – a succumbing to the illness and a relinquishment of all personal freedom and power. It would be the ultimate defeat.

We must not let that happen. We must call on the collective power of humanity. Perhaps this act of unprecedented terrorism will summon forth from the people of the world the best and brightest part of our selves that demands to be heard. That small voice in each of us that has whispered before and will no longer be ignored. The part of us that screams, *"Enough!"*

Enough hatred and contempt. Enough anger and envy. Enough poison and pills, bombs and missiles. Enough fear and resentment. Enough chasing after fortune and fame. Enough worrying and ulcers and schedules and meetings. Enough money and credit cards and new cars and clothes. Enough keeping score and weighing balances. Enough holding on to petty grievances and perceived slights. Enough nursing the wounds of the past. Enough sorrow, bitterness, and regret. *Enough is enough!*

It is time for of *all* of us – not just Americans – to stand up. It's easy to point the finger of blame and spin our theories of what could've, should've, or would've happened "if only." It's *too* easy. And too passive. The real effort begins right here. Inside. Examining our own motives. Our own hearts. To make small, daily choices that can eliminate the climate that fosters hatred and intolerance. It's time to stand up *for* something, not simply stand up *to* someone. To stand *for* peace, *for* love, *for* compassion, *for* cooperation. It's time to build something that will last.

This is not about the United States. We're just the big boy on the block. They can bomb us. They can burn us. They can batter us, but they can not bury us under the rubble of their hatred.

Now is the time.

Treasure each moment.

Choose love instead of fear.

Let's give our children something that will last.

Sifting Through the Rubble

"Sometimes even to live, is an act of courage."
—Seneca

IN THE AFTERMATH OF THE events of September 11th, there have been innumerable acts of courage and determination displayed via television and witnessed around the world, stories of hope, of faith, of loss and love. We have all of us, in some way, been affected by the falling of the twin towers.

Last weekend I visited my younger son, Andrew. He's my golfer, seventeen now and a senior in High School and though we had talked by phone and intellectually I believed he was fine, emotionally I wanted visual proof. I wanted to see him, to touch him. There is something about a tragedy that desires visual confirmation of human proximity. My heart breaks for those surviving family members of the World Trade Center victims who lack the physical reassurance of their loved ones' bodies.

I traveled to the States by car, preferring the convenience and comfort of my own vehicle, acutely aware of the increased security at the border. I was grateful for it. Along the seven-hour drive down I-81 South I listened to an audio book, "The

Great Republic," a history of the United States extrapolated from Sir Winston Churchill's *History of the English Speaking People*. I discovered that the same sense of determination and pride I experience in the lives of my family and friends flowers from the vine of independence that most vividly distinguishes Americans. The desire to conquer the vastest expanse of wilderness known to the world at the time of its discovery is now an inbred part of the collective American psyche. It was a fascinating encapsulation of my country's birth and maturation process and I found myself developing a new and deeper appreciation for my heritage.

Andrew and I had made plans to play a round of golf with my brother who also lives in Baltimore. The three of us met in the early mist of an Indian summer Saturday at a beautiful golf course in the rolling hills of northern Maryland's horse country. The first several holes it was an easy thing to track our errant shots by observing the trails left by the golf balls as they skittered across the dew covered fairways.

We talked and caught up with each other, the primary topic of conversation being our reactions to the attack. My brother had been having some difficulties with his eighteen-year old son's lackadaisical attitude. After September 11th Bill said, "We've had dinner as a family every night since. It's put things into perspective."

Andrew said he wasn't watching any news about it any more. He'd had enough. Not only was the event not a primary focus, he refused to make it one. Andrew is pretty grounded (at least most of the time). He feels, he attaches logic, he releases, he moves on. We arrived at the next hole. Andrew got out of the cart, pulled out his driver and took a few swings. He has become a young man this summer, somehow growing into his large frame.

"All these people think everybody should be all upset," he said. "I mean, sure, I'm upset. But, like, what am I supposed to do? Fall apart? Worry about it? That doesn't make any sense. How does that help anything?"

Andrew stopped swinging his club and looked at me. His eyes looked older, more direct. He lifted his left arm and made a sweeping gesture toward the trees and fairways in whose bosom we were so safely nestled. "Look around, Mom," he said. His head turned to follow his arm, his eyes taking in the beauty and stillness of our surroundings. "My life hasn't changed. I'm out here on a Saturday morning playing golf. I'm doing the same things I used to do. I see the same friends. I still go to school, still go to work, still drive. I still see you."

He was quiet for a second as he took a ball and tee from his pocket. *He lacks the context of history, the understanding time lends to life,* I thought to myself. *How can he begin to assimilate the long-term implications of this world event? Is this his way of protecting himself? Or is this an example of the American spirit? Is Andrew, at this moment, at this precious time in his life, taking the bravest course of action he knows?* My mind silently asked the questions as I watched my son.

He turned and walked toward the slightly elevated tee box, bending down to wedge his tee into the ground. He stepped behind the ball, glanced up the fairway and took a final practice swing. Looking once again to the ball, then to the fairway, he approached the ball and spoke again. "I figure the best thing I can do is just live my life."

His arms straightened as he gripped his driver and bent his knees. "Just live it," he repeated more quietly. He paused. "And whack this ball straight down the middle." He swung – over 300 yards straight down the middle. "You caught all of that one!" Bill exclaimed. "Yeah," Andrew responded with a big grin. "That one felt good."

We didn't keep score that round. We just played the game. It was about the day, it was about the people, it was about the green grass and blue sky, it was about the club selection and individual swings. It was about *this* putt, not that last one. It was about *now*, not later. It was about feelings, not performance. It was a wonderful, relaxed round of golf, almost its own paradox. It became a celebration – a declaration of independence – of our freedom of choice. As the three of us enjoyed each other's company and the beauty of our surroundings I thought of all the people who have reached out to other people, all the acts of kindness and examples of bravery evidenced in big and small ways. I felt connected to and grateful for the interdependence of all living things.

Robert F. Kennedy said, "It is from the numberless diverse acts of courage and belief that human history is shaped. Each time a man stands up for an ideal or acts to improve the lot of others or strikes out at injustice, he sends forth a tiny ripple of hope, and crossing each other from a million different centers of energy and daring those ripples build a current which can sweep down the mightiest walls of oppression and resistance." Continuing to live can feel like a betrayal, as though in our happiness we are somehow being disloyal to the memory of those affected by death, and yet it may be the greatest gift we can give each other in difficult times – the gift of hope.

I believe it. Hope is a healing thing. It is a courageous thing. It leads by example and it cheers from the sidelines of reality. Life is lonelier without it. And most importantly, hope calls forth that indomitable part of us that insists on sifting through the rubble, the part of us that still desires to conquer the wilderness.

Or the golf course.

Intangibles: The Stuff of Substance

"Giving is the secret of a healthy life. Not necessarily money, but whatever a man has of encouragement and sympathy and understanding."
—John D. Rockefeller, Jr.

I LIE IN MY BED, the end of another day, a Tuesday, just another simple Tuesday (which strikes me now as an auspicious day in recent months) and replay the day, pushing rewind in my head as I often do, examining the conversations and events and my responses to them. I sift through the day's intricacies, its potential secret places, as a buyer might open the drawers of a writing desk on the showroom floor before nodding in satisfaction and pulling out a wallet. There is something in this process that allows my mind a degree of certainty – though not necessarily permanence – to facilitate a good night's sleep. *This morning...*

This morning I am to meet a friend at the old city hall to lend support as she faces the man who defrauded, raped, and terrorized her over a two month period two and half years ago. This will be her first sighting of him since. She has asked me to be there. I have rearranged a few things to clear my day. Glancing at my calendar I notice that tomorrow and Thursday are full; Friday is blessedly blank.

I ride the subway in silence. I feel strangely calm. There is nothing rushed about the morning. There is nothing rushed about the entire day, the machinations of the court system being what they are. She is told to return on Friday. She will have an opportunity to say what she must to this man at that time. I will be there too.

I return to the Eaton Centre and the subway beneath it. An elderly gentleman, shorter than I and with an accent asks me if this is the way to the subway. On his arm is a old woman, stooped, with bright eyes and a big smile. It seems fixed in place, somehow a permanent part of my brief image of her. We enter the mammoth mall together – I hold the door – and then they are lost in the shuffle of the busy downtowners, the fleet of foot, the ones with schedules.

I find the escalator down and see the old couple walking slowly, one measured step at a time, down the stairs at an angle to the escalator. She grips his forearm as he grips the handrail. I wonder at their choice. Their progress seems painstaking.

Arriving at the entrance to the station itself in the labyrinth of underground walkways, I put my token in the box, nudge the turnstile with my hip and head to the transfer box. Pushing the button I glance up at the stream of people heading through the various steel-armed entry ways. There are a lot of people. They move quickly. They carry lots of things: book bags, back-packs, briefcases and purses; papers and coffees and gloves and food. They are a blur in their urgency to get somewhere.

Behind them the elderly couple has come into view. They do not carry anything in their hands – just each other. They look lost. I return to the turnstile and guide them to the other side. We are all heading north but find ourselves on the south side, requiring us to descend even further to wind our way across. We talk a bit as I take her frail arm and hold on fast, descending the steps as one would do with a three year old. Her husband holds her other arm. We move slowly. People collect behind us. We are slowing them down. I feel apologetic. Once at the bottom I see an up escalator to the north side. This will help her, I think. But we walk the stairs, up, one at a time, for she will no longer ride escalators. Her husband, Carl, tells me that she fell on one last year leaving her head bloodied and her spirit frightened by metal steps that move.

Her name is Teresa. She has not spoken, yet, but her smile is there still; she seems most content to be wedged between her husband and a perfect stranger, walking up a flight of stairs. We arrive at the top and await the next train. They are returning to their home in Scarborough. They have lived in the same house since they emigrated from Austria in 1957, Carl says. I can feel his pride in having provided security and consistency for so long. Carl has said very few words, really, his silent handling of so precious a cargo speaking volumes about his character and values.

Their only son is a marine biologist who lives in Tahiti. They don't see him much, Carl tells me. It's a long ways away. Carl glances away when he speaks of his son. He pauses briefly, visiting somewhere else before returning to the platform where we now stand. But his son finally married – at fifty years of age, Carl says – and they now have a two year old grand daughter. Her name is Serena. I say what a pretty name, and smile. They smile too, and nod. Teresa says, Serena, and her smile broadens. She sounds as though she may have had a stroke. Carl tells me Teresa has Alzheimer's. He looks at his wife. His eyes indicate it's getting worse, but there is no embarrassment lingering there, only tenderness.

The train arrives and we once again form our phalanx, marching one small step at a time and entering through the sliding doors of the nearest car. There are two seats together and they sit. I sit across from them. We smile at each other and say a few things, very few; it is enough to have walked together. They have told me their stop and so when it is announced I alert them and they rise, slowly, she clutching and almost falling as the car slows, he steadying her and himself. They must cross the aisle and exit the car through the doors next to my seat. I rise, more as a measure of respect than an attempt to lend assistance, and wish them both well. We know we shall not see each other again, without God's assistance.

The train halts and the doors open. Teresa turns to me and smiles. She says thank you. She says you are very kind. She says goodbye and then she and Carl move through the open doors and head toward the next staircase. I watch them melt into the crowd and smile. I feel no pity, no sorrow, rather a mixture of humility and some envy: to have lived in the same house for fifty years, with dedication and pride, with a partner, with a love, and to be headed there.

The tape recorder fast forwards. I talk to another gentleman, by phone, by chance as he calls from Edmonton. He has called his friend, in whose office I am at present after saying goodbye to Carl and Teresa. I speak to this man, faceless on the phone, and he thanks me at the end. I have somehow alleviated a concern of his.

I have dinner with another friend and my husband. This

friend has several drinks and upon arriving back to our home asks to open the bottle of wine he had brought with him. I glance at my husband and tell our friend opening the wine is fine – as long as he spends the night. You have a choice I say: wine and our guest bed, or no wine and your car. As he has already consumed enough at dinner to put himself, and potentially others, in danger should he attempt to drive home, I hope he will choose the former. He does. He seems grateful and almost visibly relaxes. I excuse myself and retire for the evening leaving the men to their talk and T.V. sports.

The tiny tape recorder snaps off. I am finished examining the nooks and crannies of my day. I realize I have accomplished nothing of tangible, measurable worth; I made no sale today, rang no bell, tallied no scorecard. I did not promote my business nor hand out a single card. I sat in a court room, held an old woman's hand, offered perspective to a stranger on the phone and reassured a friend of his worth.

Yes, it has been a very good day, indeed.

Towers, Truth and Trusting

"As children we were visionaries. We looked at the world from the highest tower in the kingdom of possibilities."
—Duane Kennedy

THERE HAS BEEN A MARKED increase in the number of participants in The Trust Program who stand at the threshold of their dreams, recoiling from the possibilities they foreshadow: the larger the dream, the higher the perspective, the greater the potential to experience vertigo. It's scary, standing at that threshold, with a dream in your heart and a penny in your pocket.

One woman has just finished her book and finds herself frozen by fear, but of what? She is about to step over that threshold, arms wide open and ready for all she's ever wanted. Yet she continues to stand there and wonders why. Another man wants to start a new idea within his company and is still "gathering the data" months later, well aware of his own procrastination strategy but unable to move forward.

Some call it fear of success. Others call it a fear of failure. I think it's more likely a fear of accountability. I think our worst fear is that we will be held accountable for the impact of our dreams. The larger the impact, the greater the potential burden of responsibility. Want to change the world? Are you prepared to shoulder it?

Think of all the leaders you admire, living or dead. I'm willing to bet that every one of them did not start out trying to change the world. They started by changing themselves and the small corner of the world in which they lived. Gandhi took a stand in South Africa before India. Jesus took a stand in the desert before Jerusalem, Mother Teresa in Calcutta, Winston Churchill in London. They began with a simple dream, a glimpse from the tower of possibilities, and continued to dare to cling to that vision, even as they came back down to the ground and did what they could where they were.

We grow into greatness one small step at a time. We grow into leadership one step at a time. The fear of our own potential is the only real stopping point for most people. As Marianne Williamson wrote in her oft-quoted piece on manifesting our potential, "It is our light, not our darkness that frightens us. We ask ourselves, 'Who am I to be brilliant, gorgeous, talented and fabulous? Actually, who are we *not* to be? We were born to make manifest the glory of God that is within us. It's not just in some of us, it's in everyone."

The sadness and regret of having turned our back on our own potential is a sword that will wound the soul. Yet, to continue to sit on the edge of that sword is its own slow death. We will either pick up our hopes and dreams, charging bravely into the land of possibilities, sword in hand, or we will witness their slow withered walk to the gallows. Goethe said, "An unused life is an early death." The choice has ever been such: to live while we die or to die while we live.

Barbara Sherr summed it up in the title of one of her books, *I Could Do Anything If Only I Knew What It Was*. I think many of us *do* know what we want to do we just don't think we can make a living doing it. Or else the price of persevering until we *can* make a living at it is seen as too steep. Or deep down we don't believe ourselves worthy of the abundance we see coming our way.

The secret is this: when we are engaged in work that causes us such joy – simply in the *doing* of whatever it is – it *is* what we are called to do. It *is* our unique contribution and it *is* our calling. And we *know* that. Deep inside we *know* it. And *that's* what so scary. To know so deeply something so clearly that the longing ache which springs forth from the very knowingness of it is its own sweet reward.

It's the same ache experienced when a parent looks into the sleeping face of their newborn child, or when they witness their first dance recital, or soccer game. It's the same deep ache produced by some great works or art or music, or the handicraft efforts of a five year old as he hands you a homemade present. It's the same ache created in the long awaited reunion with a loved one, or the sending off of one held dear. It is the ache we recognize but run from, convinced of our own unworthiness.

It is the ache of unconditional love.

This Christmas we will celebrate the birth of a child who grew up to change the world. He is said to have taught, "Unless ye become as a child ye shall not enter the kingdom of heaven." I think he was referring to a state of being as evidenced by the visionary power of children and their willingness to view life from the highest tower in the kingdom of possibilities. Maybe it is time for a few adults to join them there.

Quiet White Wonders and Love Collisions

"Love has nothing to do with what you are expecting to get – only what you are expecting to give – which is everything. What you receive in return varies. But it really has no connection with what you give. You give because you love…"
—Katharine Hepburn

CHRISTMAS WAS A QUIET THING this year. My sons were off skiing with friends so my husband and I drove to northern Illinois to spend the holidays with my youngest sister, her husband and their young daughter, my god-child, Samantha.

I had crocheted Samantha a blanket for Christmas in a rainbow of colours spending many nights this fall thinking about her as I worked away, often imagining how she might greet my gift on Christmas morning. I dared not allow myself any expectations beyond a possible appreciation for the bright conglomeration of colours. After all, she's only three and a half. I honestly expected her to say nothing beyond the obligatory, "Thank you, Aunt Cindy" uttered at the prompting of her parents. This gift was made from love, with love, and for love, and carried no "balance due." Or so I thought.

After stockings had been emptied and a bit of breakfast consumed, we began opening presents. This was Sammy's first *real* Christmas and she was *totally* engaged in the mystery of Santa's arrival and her new dress-up clothes. She ran from gift to gift in her new diaphanous white fairy dress with matching white wings, rummaging under the tree, handing out presents while commanding us to "Open *this* one now!"

She was on the verge of overload, which, as any parent knows, is a dangerous precursor to the dreaded limbo-land of "time-outs." Overload is displayed as increased motor activity accompanied by decreasing attention span complicated by massive sugar intake. If you don't catch it in time, the child can quickly morph into some sort of small, rabid dog that needs to be dragged, panting and snarling, all the way to the time out chair. Fortunately, her parents intervened, settling Samantha on the floor (*"Sit! Stay!"*), before she became unreachable by reason.

I chose that moment to retrieve the gift bag with my tissue wrapped blanket of love inside. It's funny all the thoughts that can go through one's head in a flash and odder still to notice them and watch oneself, as though the external observer, in a moment of potential learning. *If it's going to get lost in the "rush" of openings*, I thought, bending to pick it up *let it be now*. I caught myself. *Oh, no! No expectations? I thought I had no expectations! Rats! I must have expectations to have had that thought. There's a hope – A desire to have it mean something. To somehow have her recognize the love that went into making it… But wait…There's a difference between hoping and expecting… You made it in love now deliver it that way!*

I handed Sammy the bag. She opened it – slowly and deliberately – perched on her knees on the floor, and carefully laid the tissue wrapped bundle on the floor. We were all surprised by that alone. Her subsequent reaction, however, left us speechless.

"Remember the blanket I was making last summer at the River, and you helped me? Do you remember that?" I asked. Sammy had climbed into my lap last July as I had worked on another newborn's blanket and had said how pretty the colours were and how much she liked them.

Samantha looked up from the floor at me and nodded. "Well," I continued, "since you liked it so much, I made a different blanket for you out of the same colours. It's a special blanket, a love blanket." *There – that's it. No expectations.*

She began to peel away the transparent paper gently, almost reverently. I watched in wonder as someone I love laid bare my devotion. Of my own choice, in her tiny hands she held my heart.

Samantha slowly pulled off the last of the tissue paper, revealing the bright granny square creation underneath. Her mouth rounded and her hands came together under her chin in a spontaneous gesture of awe. Her eyes got very big. "*Ohhh,*" she sighed, "It's *beautiful!*" Her tiny hand brushed the blanket's surface tenderly as one would stroke a sleeping child's head. "It's the most *beautiful* blanket I *ever* saw," she said softly. "I *love* it!" She took hold of it, kneeling there on the floor, and raised it to her cheek as though hugging a stuffed animal. Closing her eyes, she gripped the blanket to her so tightly she quivered – actually *quivered!* – as love collided with love.

She was completely quiet, as were the adults in the room. We recognized the sacredness of the moment. Tears sprang to our eyes. We watched as Sammy silently raised herself from the floor and walked to the center of the room, blanket in hand. Carefully, she laid it out flat. And then she lifted one corner, climbed in under, and wrapped her self up in it.

The moment extended in stillness into eternity. The lights on the tree blinked on and off. Outside, snow fell in what can only be described as a Bing Crosby "White Christmas" sort of way, calmly, without wind to give it voice. It was a moment of shared joy, special joy – the quiet kind, without squeals or squeaks or screams – the kind, I believe, that will flash before our eyes when we die; those moments when the sweetness of life assaults us head on; moments whose touch is so sure, so strong, as to be utterly intoxicating in their power to transform and uplift; those moments when all life's intricacies and complexities are reduced to one simple explanation for any and all of our personal struggles – one single experience of complete connection.

I remember a New Year's Eve, six years ago, when I was returning to Toronto after conducting a five-day retreat. It had snowed the night before and as a friend drove us south toward the city I gazed out the passenger window at the sun setting in the west, the glory of the sky's sweeping strokes of magenta and yellow reflected in the pristine winter-white landscape. Tears sprang to my eyes and I asked my friend to pull over to the side of the road for a minute to witness the sheer splendor available to us on this deserted country lane. We sat there, in quiet, and watched the sun sink behind the edge of the horizon, too moved to speak. It was, and still is, one of the purest moments of sheer joy I have ever experienced.

I think we all crave those moments. We crave them so much we try to create them with planning and purchasing and expectations. Moments like that – truly joyful moments – come as a result of *not* trying to create them. Rather they come from being *present* for them – to notice them. They're all around us, everyday. Are some sweeter than others? Are some easier to recognize? Sure. Moments like the one with Sammy just make it easier to remember the real message of Christmas: that when we create *with* love and give *from* love we receive more than we ever dreamed possible.

May life offer you gifts far beyond your greatest expectations, and may you find the stillness needed to notice them.

Trail Markers and Soul Whispers

"In the depth of your hopes and desires lies your silent knowledge of the beyond. And like seeds dreaming beneath the snow your heart dreams of spring. Trust those dreams, for in them is hidden the gate to eternity."
—Kahlil Gibran

MY YOUNGEST SISTER, JENNIFER, WHO had drawn my name this year in the annual family secret Santa, gave me two sets of sheets for our new Queen size, deep pocket mattress. These quality cotton coverings were much appreciated, the result of my more practical middle sister's suggestion, and a good one at that.

The larger gift was accompanied by a few smaller items: some candles and a holder, a photo album with cut out stars on its silver and black velvet cover and a small book that had once been mine that Jenny had stumbled across while cleaning out some old boxes.

I looked at the cover, a weathered green with worn corners, and recognized the title: *Now We Are Six,* by A.A. Milne. Opening it I saw my mother's familiar and fluid penmanship: "For Cindy, on your sixth birthday – With love from Mother and

Daddy." I started flipping through the pages as image wisps from a far away time crept to the fringe of my memory. I had obviously spent a great deal of time with this book. I remembered many of the delightful poems.

Continuing to turn the pages *something* began to stir inside me. Something elusive and fleeting like a wisp of a delicious restaurant aroma sniffed from a moving vehicle in a bustling city; or the dream that fades incompletely upon awakening, but enough so that it can't quite be remembered either. As I made my way through words that had once been so well known I became more and more fascinated. I heard Jenny remark that if she'd known how much I'd enjoy the book she could've skipped the sheets. And then I was lost, traveling through time as if in some kind of soundproof room.

I looked at the illustrations, simple but detailed pen and ink images and started to recognize old friends. I went back to the table of contents and examined them more closely. Apparently I – or an errant crayon clutching younger sibling – had attempted to clarify the page numbers assigned to each poem in the contents by carefully, though not very accurately, drawing a red crayon from the poem name on the left side of the page to its corresponding page number on the right hand side. In addition, someone had circled certain poem titles in pencil. The contents covered two pages and there were four titles circled on the first page, four on the second, eight in all. I read the first few of these, and these – *ah, these* – I remembered. *These* poems I knew. These, like an old pair of jeans found in the bottom of a drawer, still fit!

It was then that I began wondering why *those* eight poems would have been circled and in particular, the fifth one at the top of the second page, entitled "Little Black Hen." This circle had been grayed in by pencil, with a tiny arrow pointing down to it from above with the word "this" written in above the arrow. It seemed to have been distinctly singled out from the others. I found this most curious and so I read the poem more carefully. I had begun to wonder whether I had left myself some sort of map, a code, a set of very important directions from an age when my heart had been a bit purer than it now is, less blurred by time, less jaded by pain.

I spent some time – how long exactly I could not tell you – attempting to make sense of a six year olds' reasoning and finally decided I was reading *way* too much into these circled titles. I closed the book rather forcefully and put it face down beside me.

And that's when I saw it. On the back cover had been drawn, in pencil, a series of seven stars in varying sizes. The largest star was in the upper right hand corner of the back cover. Two inches to its left was another larger star, and again, two inches below it was another, forming an almost perfect equilateral triangle in the upper right corner. The remaining smaller stars were scattered within the perimeter of the larger triangle – appearing to be after thoughts of lesser importance.

The past and present collided and I smiled to myself even as a shudder of recognition ran through me. I had been complicating a very simple matter searching among circled titles for clues from the past. Staring me in the face was a replica of my current (and only) company logo; three shooting stars reflecting the same formation a six year had drawn on the back of her favourite book over forty years ago.

It is said that the seeds of our authentic self, the person we yearn to become, are to be found in the simplest, everyday acts and the natural easy stuff of our childhood. Psychologist and author James Hillman describes what he calls his "acorn theory" in *The Soul's Code*: in the acorn lies the DNA of the future oak. It doesn't look that way to the naked eye, but somehow the acorn knows itself to be an oak, not an elm or maple, and grows to become one. Hillman states, "The acorn theory proposes and I will bring evidence for the claim that you and I and every single person is born with a defining image... Still, the innate image of your [calling] holds all in the co-presence of today, yesterday, and tomorrow...You are that essential image that develops, if it does. As Picasso said, 'I don't develop; I am.'"

Carl Jung declared image to be psyche. Imagery – whether expressed through painting, singing, or writing – is the language of the unconscious. In *Healing Fiction* Hillman goes on to suggest that the images with which we most resonate hold the clearest clues to our souls' calling. He writes, "When I ask, 'Where is my soul, how do I meet it, what does it want now?' the answer is, "Turn to your images." Gregg Levoy, insightful author of *Callings: Finding and Following an Authentic Life* concurs. "To some degree," he writes, "an image *does* capture soul, but more likely the soul of the person who *created* it."

When I formed my company all I had was an idea for a new program designed to help people learn how to trust themselves, others and the process of life in general so as to be better able to deal with – indeed, to thrive in the midst of – life's inherent anxieties. When it came time to pick a name for my little fledgling business, I chose the name "Constellation" only because of a mechanism in the program itself – a physical process of compiling the key people, places, events and decisions of a person's life and actually sticking a bunch of different stars on a sheet of blue paper to indicate the most important ones, thereby forming a "Life Constellation." Originally intended only as a right brain creative activity, a break from all the logical data gathering exercises, the process has since become the legs on which the Trust Program stands. It is magical: it somehow transforms people and the vision they have of their lives.

But I did not know that when I chose the name. It was just a name. Unable to identify what it is that I *do* at that point in my development any name would suffice. Later, when incorporating, I needed to isolate a more specific version of "Constellation," there being many companies with that word in their name. I chose "Learning" because it was a) available; b) came closest to summarizing what we're about; and c) ended the name choosing process of which I was well tired by then.

Six months before I actually left my former employer in February 1998, a participant in one of the classes I taught at the time and owner of an international design company called to offer his expertise. "When you're ready to leave – and you will – I'd like to design your logo for you." He designed several versions on the basis of a one-page description of the Trust Program. I chose the final version: three stars in triangle formation shooting up and off to the right.

Since that time I have on occasion thought of the rather haphazard way in which the name and our resulting icon came to be. Perhaps, I thought, I should bring a specialist on board to come up a better name. I adore the logo. However, in this age of personal branding a company name, so I'm told, should present at a glance what we stand for, and Constellation Learning, Inc. doesn't quite fall into that category.

One day a young girl daydreamed and doodled on the back of a book, leaving a trail marker – a bit of ribbon tied to a branch along the path – for the woman she would become. And the wind passed and the ribbon whispered a gentle bit of encouragement from the sidelines of the past, confirming the present, and inviting an invitation to look to the future stars yet to be reached.

Dear God,

Whose omnipresent compassion is at the heart of all creation, I thank you with deep humility that you should love me as I am and still invite me to become every day a fuller expression of your mercy and grace. I stand in awe of the Universal capacity to communicate and inspire. I have come full circle only to find I never left the little girl I was, and am still.

And I thank you – for loving me, for inspiring me, for guiding me and bringing me ever closer to you. I thank you for the work that I do and the people with whom I am blessed to do it. I thank you for your endless sense of humour and most especially for the recognition of the unique calling that is mine and yours in laughing, dancing unity.

May it last for all eternity and may we, together, dance among the stars.

On Holy Ground

"The kingdom of God is within."
—Jesus of Nazareth, Mohammed, Buddha, Lao Tzu
and every lasting voice from recorded history

IT IS EASTER MORNING AND a gloriously sunny day. The thermometer reads almost sixty degrees, positively balmy by Canadian standards. I sit at my desk and type while gazing out on a backyard bursting forth from its winter bondage. The purple crocuses are awake and the daffodils stand at alert for imminent opening. All of nature screams "new life!" while Bach's *Jesu, Joy of Man's Desiring* plays softly beside me.

All over the continent little girls are wearing special Easter dresses while mothers attempt to contain unruly little boys in rarely worn navy blue jackets. Earlier today some of these children hunted for jelly beans and eggs and in some cases awakened to a basket with coloured strands of cellophane grass containing a large chocolate bunny. Later it's off to various forms of worship and on to family gatherings. These are Easter traditions and rituals from my Judeo-Christian upbringing. It is a point of reference in my life, a way of seeing it, a way of translating its mystery into common experience.

Passover and Easter trumpet in spring with a promise of new

life. Much of the world is celebrating the mystery of life today, though they may do it in different ways.

There was a time when I would have felt a certain (for lack of a better commonly understood word) embarrassment; of being somehow disrespectful by not attending a church service, for not appearing in a holy house of God, on such a day as Easter. I do not experience that feeling now. For me the holy house of God is this earth, this sky, the water that nourishes and the air that sustains, and the living, breathing creatures for which it does so.

I remember my father referring to all the good "twice-a-year-Christians" he saw in church every Easter Sunday. He meant those who appeared at the high feast days because *not* to do so would be a social faux pas more than a spiritual one. I remember not wanting to be one of those people, the implication being that their relationship with the Almighty was in jeopardy. Or at least that was a little girl's interpretation of my father's words. Upon reflection, I think he may have been expressing his sadness for those people rather than his judgment of them.

I think that's how God must feel sometimes (to continue the universal human tendency to anthropomorphize something beyond our capacity to contain, control, or comprehend). I think He just shakes his head sometimes and says, "Thanks for coming by, and now, when you leave this place you built in order to acknowledge Me, please remember that I go with you. Acknowledge Me wherever you are for I am everywhere and always around and with and in you. All is sacred."

Rituals and traditions are a necessary part of human existence. Indeed, they are a necessary part of our development, individually and collectively. They spring from a deep human need to understand and connect. It is when the rituals themselves begin to take on more significance than the philosophical foundations and belief structures on which they were based that we find ourselves feeling pulled. A piece of us wants to believe, another says "tomorrow, it'll be business as usual."

It doesn't have to be.

Many years ago I watched an old television special of an interview with the architect Frank Lloyd Wright by Mike Wallace of "60 Minutes" fame. Known for his ground-breaking designs and incorporation of natural settings into those designs, Wright was also a deep thinker with an irreverent sense of humor, two human traits for which I have a fondness. I remember only one thing from the interview besides the fact that it was in black and white and that Mike Wallace smoked on camera (both a reflection of the times). Mike said, "You call yourself a spiritual man, yet you no longer attend church of any kind."

It is Wright's response I remember most vividly. As the camera switched over to him, this elderly, soft-spoken man paused and a small smile came to his face. "Ah," he replied, "I can understand your dilemma. If you think God is to be only found in church, then you'll miss Him everywhere else. I am in church whenever I take a walk in the woods, or design a home, or speak to another human being. Holy ground exists wherever you create it."

We are invited, every single day, to acknowledge holy ground, to see the gifts of Life around and with and in us. Today, find a tree, or a crocus, or sit still in the sun for a moment, or look into the eyes of a small child open to life in all its glorious absurdities, or listen to music, or sing, or call a friend, or laugh out loud, or skip down the street, or smile at the person sitting across from you on the bus. We cannot celebrate what we do not notice. Celebrate life in whatever way causes you to feel inspired by its mystery and majesty. Awe can be the gateway to an experience of heaven on earth.

I leave you with the words of another man, Joseph Campbell, who understood the human need for myth, magic and marvel. "This fear of the unknown, this free-fall into the future," Campbell writes in *Thou Art That*, "can be detected all around us. But we live in the stars and we are finally moved by awe to our greatest adventures. The kingdom of God is within us."

May you be aware of that today and every day, and may this month prove to be a great adventure for you, full of awe.

Balance Sheets and Creative Accounting

> "Not everything that can be counted, counts – and not everything that counts can be counted."
> —Albert Einstein

DURING THE AMAZING WEEK OF warm weather that awakened spring recently here in Ontario I had the great good fortune to be leading The Trust Program on the edge of South Lake near Kingston. The participants and I wandered about in shorts and were witness to that fleeting time each spring when the red-hued buds burst forth, peeling back their protective outer layers to display the remarkable new-born green heralding spring's arrival in a bolder way than any crocus ever could.

I felt tremendously blessed. Being so present in so secluded a spot at just the right time was a fluke: the program dates are selected months in advance. A nice perk to my job, I thought on the drive back to Toronto, and the second year in a row that we've managed to pre-select the exact week of warmth that coaxed forth the trees.

This time frame also trumpets the arrival of another anxiously awaited annual event: income taxes. In the States the day has come and gone. Here in Canada, yesterday was a busy day for a lot of people and I suspect not an entirely pleasant one for some. It seems spring demands us to clean house and shed our own husks of protection as do the tree buds.

There's a great story that's been around for awhile. I've used it in my programs and with teams for over ten years as a way to illustrate the more positive aspects of expansion when one is caught in the apparent difficulties of the change itself. It goes like this:

> "A man found a cocoon of the emperor moth and took it home to watch it emerge. One day a small opening appeared, and for several hours the moth struggled but couldn't seem to force its body past a certain point.
>
> Deciding something was wrong, the man took scissors and snipped the remaining bit of cocoon. The moth emerged easily, its body large and swollen, the wings small and shriveled. He expected that in a few hours the wings would spread out in their natural beauty, but they did not. Instead of developing into a creature free to fly, the moth spent its life dragging around a swollen body and shriveled wings.
>
> The constricting cocoon and the struggle necessary to pass through the tiny opening are God's way of forcing fluid from the body into the wings. The 'merciful' snip was, in reality, cruel. Sometimes the struggle is exactly what we need."
>
> *from "Leadership," shared by Quote Magazine in 1990*

I think about a couple of coaching clients and the issues with which they are currently dealing. I think of recent (and even long ago) program participants and their struggles. I think of my own "husk-shedding" as well as my children's. Struggle may be just what we "need" as did the emperor moth, but it sure doesn't feel that way to him, I bet, as he's laying there exhausted, half in and half out of his cocoon! I wonder if those tree buds experience struggle as they open up to the world?

There are women waiting to find Mr. Right or to have a baby; there are men waiting for a promotion, and young adults waiting to get into universities. The whole of humanity is sometimes half in and half out of their individual cocoons. And a lot of it shows in the spring, I've discovered, because just like animals and plants, much of humanity hibernates over the winter. Perhaps we are supposed to. Perhaps spring invites human sprouting as much as any plant.

So spring's awakening, as well as our own, coincides with tax time each year to remind us that there are lots of balance sheets in life. Numbers reflect one sheet. Family reflects another. Friendships display still another, as do countless other aspects of life that are just as real, though perhaps not so visible, as numbers seem to be at this time of year. Even Einstein had trouble with numbers, believe it or not, when it came to tax time. "The hardest thing in the world to understand," he said, "is income tax." As my accountant reminds me, there's lots of ways to be creative. It all depends on what you want.

There are many balance sheets in life.

The trick is in the tallying.

Charity from the Inside Out

> "A man may bestow great sums on the poor and indigent without being charitable, and may be charitable when he is not able to bestow anything."
> —Joseph Addison

A BOSTON NEWS STATION REPORTED the findings of a recent study that measured the charitable giving levels across the United States. The results showed that New Englanders, according to the local news anchor who reported the findings, "live up to their reputation of stinginess" by giving the least amount to charities. She went on to explain that "of course, this study did not include church donations," implying that not all New Englanders – and certainly not Bostonians, with their staunch Roman Catholic roots – are to be included.

I smiled at her add-on explanation; perhaps she herself pledged to a church. *You're talking to a PK,* I thought. That's a "Preacher's Kid" for you lay people. I grew up in the household of a man for whom fundraising was the better part of his job description, second only perhaps to tending to his parishioners which involved performing liturgies, managing staff, outreach programs and Sunday School classes, the support of which depended on the annual giving of the congregation. Running a church is a business. When my Dad retired as an Episcopal priest he actually went to work for one of the world's largest fund-raising companies. Aside from the fact that there are even funded studies of this nature, the question of what constitutes charity and how to track it seems fruitless, really, for how does one measure the givers' intent?

In 1988 my former husband and I and our two small boys were driving through downtown Baltimore when our car was hit broad-side by a stolen vehicle speeding away from a crime scene. We were at a large intersection waiting for the light to change. When it turned green we proceeded through. Suddenly and without warning, from our left came a car speeding through the intersection with the police in silent pursuit. We were slammed across the two right lanes of traffic and into the curb.

The impact of the crash spun the car around and left us frightened and in shock. We were fortunate, though my ex-husband had a bloody nose from the airbag release and, it turned out, I had broken a rib. I noticed three things very distinctly as we piled out of the car and checked to make sure we were all OK. The first was that the vehicle that had struck us was perhaps fifty feet away and had run right up onto the sidewalk with a police car right behind it. Both cars stood empty. The perpetrators had fled on foot and the police had given chase.

The second thing I noticed was that all the other cars on the street were slowly and carefully driving *around* our smashed up car; not a single one stopped as we stood there helplessly, my ex husband bleeding profusely through his fingers. We had nothing with which to cover his nose to stem the blood.

It was then that I noticed two very scruffy looking men walking toward us, one much taller than the other. It being a Sunday there was no one else on the street. They were perhaps a hundred feet away. I turned from them, hoping they wouldn't approach, *they probably want a hand out,* I thought, and attempted to find some Kleenex or a rag or *something* in the car, to no avail.

When I straightened up from my search the two homeless men, dressed in tatters, were now upon us, perhaps twenty feet away. They walked slowly, hesitantly, much as a child might approach an animal it longs to pet but fears might bite. The taller one held out his hand; in it he held a large wad of napkins the kind one gets at McDonald's. He said not a word but continued to walk toward us offering the wad of paper in our time of distress.

He looked me in the eyes that last twenty feet, and I looked at him. I *really* looked at him. Even now I can picture his clear blue eyes and the kindness they radiated; eyes that had seen pain, a heart that knew compassion. I took the napkins from his hand – *his fingernails were so dirty and broken* – and verbalized my profuse thanks, much of which was reiterated to assuage the guilt I felt regarding my previous inaccurate and uncharitable thoughts. But even then I was graced to notice it all, to realize my short-sightedness and to learn from it. I shy away from no scruffy street person now; I look them in the eyes--and remember.

Mother Teresa was once quoted as saying, "Charity, to be fruitful, must cost us." I think she meant that a truly charitable act costs our *heart*, not necessarily our pocket book. The cost is the stretching of the heart muscle with a daily workout. When we extend ourselves to others, reach out and help the old man crossing the street when we're running late to an appointment, or let the other guy out into traffic ahead of us; when we smile and don't reply with a deadly one-liner to the annoying co-worker or misbehaving child; when we stop and listen to what our spouse is attempting to say even when we "know" they're wrong; when we actually smile at someone who looks lonely or ask if we can help the one who looks lost – these are acts of charity. A charitable *heart* determines the qualification of a charitable *gift*.

We are not all called to give large sums of money. Money is an external measuring stick, a tangible one. Writing a check is a thousand times quicker and easier than addressing the resentments, condemnations and animosities that may live inside our hearts. When we give from the heart, it *does* cost us – and it's usually our pride and arrogance.

When I think of true charity, I remember a tall, tattered, blue-eyed stranger who once handed me all his napkins.

Finding the Soft Spot of Safety

"When one has made his demands of the Universal, he must be ready for surprises. Everything may seem to be going wrong, when in reality, it is going right."
—Florence Scovel Shinn

LOVE IS NOT AN ABSTRACT term. It invites choices and some of those choices may be accompanied by feelings other than the warm and mushy, highly touted Hallmark variety. We can think we've made things worse sometimes, when in reality we've set into motion a healing process necessary for future growth. It's like seeking advice after years of chronic pain: the Universe is a kindly doctor.

My brother is an orthopedic surgeon in the U.S. People come to him to fix their broken bones. They are usually in pain when they arrive. After an operation, which addresses the problem and reduces the pain, the patient must go through extensive physiotherapy so that their body actually heals. It is the healing process that can seem so taxing, so hard, and that's when we doubt the choice to have gone to the doctor in the first place.

It is an interesting time in human development. We are being asked to dig new foundations, to lay new bricks and to re-build a way of life that seems now long gone. Everywhere we look old paradigms are crumbling, old assumptions being erased with a sniper's bullet or a president's signature.

When I was six years old I walked with my friends to school each day. It took about twenty minutes to walk one way. I know of no parent today who would allow their six-year old to walk that far without an adult in attendance.

So where is one to find the strength, indeed the courage, to choose to greet life daily, as it is now, not as it *should've* been, or *could've* been, or *would've* been *if only*, with appreciation and gratitude?

An interesting question and arguably one of the most important a person will answer. People spend lifetimes searching for that answer. Along the way they either bump into themselves or they avoid the meeting; if they choose the latter, so much the sadder. If the former, they will not only discover who they are and why they're here, they will also bump into and merge with the collective whole of the Universal experience and find peace within the chaos.

To those who seek that place of peace, that soft spot of safety, look within and you will see that things are going very right indeed. Just not the way you planned.

Thank God.

Mountains, Milestones and Memories

"Sooner or later we all discover that the important moments in life are not the advertised ones, not the birthdays, the graduations, the weddings, not the great goals achieved. The real milestones are less prepossessing. They come to the door of memory unannounced, stray dogs that amble in, sniff around a bit, and simply never leave. Our lives are measured by these."
—Susan B. Anthony

MONDAY MORNING, JULY 1, 2002.

I sit in my new office and gaze out the window at nothing but green. The sun is shining and a light breeze dances through the trees, acres of them. The gardens have been turned and planted with bright splotches of colour and a new hammock lends an appearance of readiness for those who will come to this healing place in the future.

I hear nothing but the yawning of the birds and the stretching of the trees awakening to the day. There is nothing else to assault my ears: no sirens, or car horns, no shuddering buses or drone of streetcars. No dogs barking from square enclosures passing as yards, no sounds of doors opening and closing, no footsteps on the sidewalk, no place to go, no where to be, no one to see. No program to prepare, no box to unpack, no call to make: There are no to do's today.

I have waited a long time to feel this settled. My body is tired to the bone from the weeks of physical labour demanded to make the move to this piece of heaven, but my heart is at peace. Like a root-bound plant too long restricted by its environment, I feel re-potted in fertile soil: my mind is fluid with new ideas and dreams for the future.

This new soil comes at a price. It has been fertilized with the blood, sweat and tears of the past. There were many mountains to climb, many decisions made, many things left behind along the way. I am again reminded that on any journey the shedding of the unnecessary is equally as important, if not more so, than the taking on of that which is necessary.

I have had reason to review that journey recently. Not only did we move two weeks ago to South Lake, the new home of The Trust Program, I completed the physical time-line of the homeopathic sequential healing process (managing somehow to time the emotional oozing of my physical birth on the same day of the move! A truly memorable experience for anyone within ten feet of me). We also traveled to Baltimore in early June for my son's high school graduation.

It has been a busy month.

Andrew, my younger son, my baby, will turn eighteen on July 6th. To commemorate this auspicious day I compiled a scrap book of his life, a retrospective that developed its own themes rather than a chronological accounting of the passage of time. It became, as did his elder brother's who received one on his eighteenth birthday, a summary of who he is – his essence – as told through pictures and my artwork. I have had great fun with this project and was very grateful to have had the good sense to start it months in advance.

In addition to the always stimulating design aspects inherent in a project of this kind, I found two things quite interesting as I meandered through eighteen years of my son's history: 1) how the tell-tale signs of the future adult were quite evident in the early candid photos of a very young boy, and 2) how few regrets I have concerning the choices that contributed to his development.

Andrew spent a few days visiting the 1000 Islands last weekend with a couple of friends. He has grown into a gregarious, generous man, kind and easy to be with. His eyes sparkle and he is confident in who he is. He loves to share what he loves with people he loves. *I remember...*

When he was seven we often went to an indoor sports facility where you could play all sorts of games and win points in the form of tickets. Andrew and his friends collected these tickets which could be redeemed for various prizes kept under glass at the center.

One rainy Saturday morning he coaxed me into taking him there to redeem the 7500 points worth of tickets he had amassed. It was a tidy sum and had taken him months to collect so great a fortune. I recall not wanting to go. There was always a lot of "Mommy, watch this!" in those days. Upon our arrival I thought he'd try to sweet talk me into a few quarters with which to play a couple of games, but he went straight to the counter. Much to my surprise, and after quite a lot of careful consideration, he chose a tiny rose marble clock with a one inch diameter face. He asked me if I liked it. I told him I thought it was beautiful, but what about the other toys? This was a delicate and lovely time-piece and carried a price tag of 7000 points. Wouldn't he rather get something more, well, fun? I tried to talk him out of it. He was calmly, sweetly adamant. The clock it was.

What I remember most about that moment, this stray dog, was the sheer joy his small face radiated as he counted out his 10 point tickets – lots and lots of them – and the cashier pulled the clock from its shelf, passing it across the counter to his out stretched arm. He took it in his little hand and held it out to me, face beaming. It's for you he said. You can keep it on your desk so you'll always know what time it is. *And how much I love you*, I thought. That clock sits on my desk right now. It is one of my most prized possessions and reminds me everyday not only of my son and our love, but also of the joy of sharing what one has earned honestly.

My niece Samantha left yesterday with her parents to return to Chicago. She stayed with us for three nights as her Mommy and Daddy spent a few days celebrating their 15th wedding anniversary alone. At four years of age she is a constant ball of energy moving at the speed of light. She is a delight. She is all consuming. She is exhausting. Watching her engage in life in fifth gear brought back memories of Andrew at the same age. He loved sports of any kind. She loves to dance. Indeed, we had a ballet recital, the two of us on the lawn, in our ballerina outfits created by Sammy. Was that dance evidence of the future woman she is already? Were those pointed toes the nose of a new dog to take shape over the years?

June was a month of milestones. It was the last push, the full expenditure of all that was left of energy and will to reach the peak now within view. As I catch my breath, I wonder about new mountains still hidden in the clouds and the memories to be created in the climb toward them.

Meanwhile, today, I am savoring the present and enjoying the view. I intend to refill my mug, amble outside, sip my coffee on the deck and spend a few moments petting stray dogs.

They make great company.

Promoting a Platform for Peace

"The real voyage of discovery consists not in seeking new landscapes but in seeing with new eyes."
—Marcel Proust

I AM CURRENTLY PONDERING THE word 'reverence' – an offshoot of my respect related meanderings. I think that to revere someone (or thing) has a touch more 'awe' to it than simple respect. It exceeds admiration, though that's a part of it. It's a twisty little road and though it generally leads me back to the 'love" word, I quite enjoy the scenic detours.

Are reverence and reference somehow linked when it comes to global peace? I look at the various warring factions around the world and wonder how such divergent cultures, values, and varying forms of acceptable behaviours can possibly find a meeting ground of mutual tolerance. Ireland, the Middle East, Afghanistan, so many dead, so many miserable. Heavens! The U.S. and Canada even, as *friends*, promote collective stereotypes and misconceptions about each other.

If the world was one large corporation, the direct costs in human life from all our wars, poverty and ignorance would have been deemed far too expensive and the indirect costs would have bankrupted us. All the anger and fear, the worry and anxiety, the guilt and resentment, come straight off the bottom-line.

Why do so many people feel that way? How can we find peace in the world if we are unable to locate it within ourselves? Could it be the lack of an individual, personal 'due north' – that point of reference from which we each view ourselves, the world, and our place in it? Without it we wander through life like a broken compass. How can we revere something for which we have no point of reference?

Until we seek, find, and actually live an individual 'due north,' how likely is it that we will create a collective one? Corporate words fall flat in the face of individual incongruence. Just look at Enron. Or Livent. Or Nortel. Or the front page of any business section.

The opportunities to develop a personal Due North within are all around us. Everyday they are there, in front of us: in the eyes of a child, the wagging tail of a dog, a daisy in the field. Everything's a miracle. Everything.

We dilute the potential power of everyday miracles by seeking some sort of glorious revelation of the Divine – a blinding light of transcendent truth in which we would know all things and find utter peace at last. Perhaps peace begins by cultivating a sense of reverence for self, life and the connection between the two. Perhaps freedom means modeling it and joy means living of it.

I suspect that the way to contentment and peace is the same as it's ever been: seek it first in yourself. Then model it for others.

And call it love.

Creating Christmas all Year Long

"When life seems jolly rotten there's something you've forgotten, and that's to laugh and smile and dance and sing."
—Eric Idle of Monty Python

DECEMBER WAS A QUIET TIME this year. I made no mall trips, no frantic last minute shopping. I stayed at South Lake, baked cookies and rolled beeswax candles as gifts. I spent five days here, in silence mostly, with the exception of John Denver and the Muppets singing Christmas carols, an unlikely marriage but an endearingly sentimental passage into the holiday season for me.

I sang along, danced about, and brought to mind the people for whom I was baking. I got out my mothers' recipe for cutout cookies and employed childhood training at my father's side for the rolling of the candle wax. I could almost hear my departed Dad whispering warnings from the past, *"It's all in the start – a nice, parallel start when you roll. Keep the pressure even."*

Yes, it has been a joyful season and one which I noticed was very different from previous years. It was calm. It was peaceful. There were no expectations, no massive, often tension filled preparations for large family gatherings. As I age and – more significantly — as I employ more of what I teach, I have noticed a diminishment of feeling 'special' days are indeed any more special than others.

My own birthday in November seemed just another day, a day to give thanks, just like any other day. December 25th felt no different from December 15th or September for that matter. I did have my own ceremony, one way I acknowledge the Divine, kneeling in front of a large picture window and gazing out onto a clear, star-filled sky on Christmas Eve. I acknowledged the reason for the day, the birth of a man who changed the course of human history. I counted my blessings. I pictured the people most dear to me in my minds' eye and sent them love.

Birthdays, anniversaries, Mother's Day, Father's Day, Christmas, and Easter — the list of retail requirements is endless nowadays. I suspect a lot of people buy a lot of physical gifts on these arbitrarily assigned days as a way to compensate for their lack of emotional investment in their relationships during the rest of the year. If we were to treat everyday as a "special" day, would not the actual earmarked special day simply become an extension of an already cherished relationship? If, for example, one were to treat one's child or spouse as though *each day* was their birthday with all the uniqueness that implies, would not the child or spouse come to understand and internalize that they were indeed special and require less 'proof' of that fact?

I am coming to believe that the earmarking of certain days during which one is to be "nicer" can actually perpetuate feelings of separation from instead of connection to those we hold most dear. This is not true for all, but for some, with their sense of let-down during the holidays, it becomes apparent that some gifts are loaded with expectations from the giver. The let-down is evidence of those unmet expectations.

We hear all the time things like, "People are nicer at Christmas time. They hold doors open for each other. I wish we could keep this 'goodwill to man' feeling all year." We can. It's as simple as choosing it. It's as simple as saying "I'm going to pretend today is Christmas, or my own birthday!" The nice thing about this game is that no one else needs to play along or even know that I'm involved in my own little 'day celebration.'

Today is New Year's Day, yet another special day in that it denotes the beginning of a new calendar year. My wish for all of you who may be reading this newsletter:

May today and everyday from now be as special to you as your own birthday. May this year prove to be one of balance, peace, hope, and love for all.

And may you remember to laugh and smile and dance and sing.

Every single day.

Both Sides of Hope

> "Hope is definitely not the same thing as optimism. It is not the conviction that something will turn out well, but rather the certainty that something makes sense, regardless of how it turns out."
> —Vaclav Havel, former president of the Czech Republic

WAR HAS BEGUN.

I caught CNN while in Toronto mid-month and learned far more about it than I really cared to know. The night my husband and I chose to watch the news was the same day Elizabeth Smart, a teenage girl kidnapped and held captive for almost a year, had been found and returned to her family in Salt Lake City. It had happened just an hour previous and the news program devoted itself to the odds-defying report of her "miraculous" recovery nine months after being abducted from her own bedroom at knifepoint. Indeed, the word "miracle" was repeated over and over again. So were the words, "prayers," "God," "grateful," "safe," "love," and "hope." Her family declared over and over, "We never lost hope."

I've considered that word quite a bit over the years while examining the differences between hope, faith and trust. It's a loaded word. Emily Dickinson called it "a thing with feathers that perches in the soul," and Alexander Pope claimed it "springs eternal in the human breast." British writer Samuel Johnson (1709-1784) speculated that "hope is itself a species of happiness, and perhaps, the chief happiness this world affords."

But not everyone agrees. A fellow program leader once told me he thought that hanging out in hope too long was the same thing as staying a victim: consider abused spouses. H. L. Mencken labeled hope "a pathological belief in the occurrence of the impossible." Even the great American playwright, Henry Miller, called it "a bad thing. It means that you are not what you want to be. It means that a part of you is dead, if not all of you. It means that you entertain illusions. It's a sort of spiritual clap, I should say." Whew!

Apparently Samuel Johnson recognized there's a flip side to hope. "But, like all other pleasures immoderately enjoyed," he went on to say, "the excesses of hope must be expiated by pain; and expectations improperly indulged must end in disappointment."

Yup. Hope is one of those words that can start a fight. Sort of like "peace."

I believe there are essentially two aspects of hope: hope that *protects*, and hope that *propels*. Two sides of the same coin designed to counteract despair and most effective when utilized together. Hope probably protected Elizabeth Smart even as it propelled her family to find her. However, taking either side to an extreme can create martyrs or vigilantes.

Suicide bombers are a common occurrence. Someone jumped to his death from the San Francisco Bridge in protest of the war. Did he see his act as a declaration of personal belief? Or was it an act of despair?

I don't think that the absence of hope necessarily equals

despair. On the contrary, I think despair can be disabled by the space created when "protective" hope exits and "propelling" hope enters. It can create the courage to continue. I like the thought expressed by the 17th century French playwright Pierre Corneille. "My sweetest hope" he wrote, "is to lose hope."

In the same way as courage is not necessarily the absence of fear but action in the face of it, hope is not necessarily the absence of doubt but the conviction that all is well *despite* present circumstances. This attitude requires a larger perspective than the immediacy of one's daily life and the myopic self-centered interests it so often spawns.

As the Middle East erupts, I am holding fast to a trust that it all makes sense even if I am unable to discern it, no matter how it turns out.

Welcome back, Elizabeth.

Peace.

A Mid-point: Mortality Awareness

November 5, 2003

I am fifty years old today. Fifty years. What does that mean?

It means I'm only five years from early retirement and from qualifying for Medicare. It means I wear high heels as infrequently as possible and have come to enjoy elastic waistbands. How did this happen? When did this happen?

It means my body is beginning to deteriorate on a visible level. Last night at dinner the waitress was genuinely shocked – her response to hearing my age too quick to be anything other than real. "You sure don't look fifty," she said. But I see it. And just what is fifty supposed to look like? Or feel like?

I feel distant and apart from everyone. Like a glass bubble has sucked me into its center and I see and hear my life in muted tones. I find myself doubting all the choices I made that brought me here, choices I thought were in alignment with Your desires. I think this is what You meant when you said, "You must go into the wilderness." I confused it with the form – South Lake in isolation. Now I understand it to be an emotional wilder-ness.

And then I go to the comparison game: look at all those who are worse off than you, you whiny little baby! Then it's "the count your blessings" game where I find that if I died tomorrow I've left enough of myself behind in the lives and hearts of others to have counted for something. But is that enough? It used to be. Not now. Now it feels like I'm playing small. I feel called to a larger arena and have not a clue how to proceed.

Except to write. And continue to do more of what I've done before. And look where that's brought me. Sitting here crying about what I'm not exactly sure, but a sort of sadness about something I am unable to articulate clearly.

Perhaps for the first time I am feeling my own mortality, that that which I have already experienced now outweighs that which I am still to experience. So I come back to the question: what does it mean to have lived fifty years?

It means I have seen fifty winters and fifty summers. It means that I have witnessed the birth of children and the death of loved ones. It means there are people who love me and believe in me and tell me so. It means that I have come to see that there is no normal, no somewhere else I am supposed to be, no something else I'm supposed to do. There is only the here and now.

I am alive. I am human. I breathe. I cry.

I am alone in my experience of today, even as I share its arrival with others. Today, the glass wall screams 'no entry' to them. Today is my day to do what I choose.

I am tired of being the beacon for everyone else. I am beaten by the elements in my search to break new ground. I am worn out by the questions, burnt out by the stories, crushed by the weight of the pain of self-knowledge, mown down by the enormity of the *task before me.*

What I see most are all the faults, all the ways I've disappointed myself, the ways I've not stepped up to the plate, the times I've let others down. I look in the mirror and see a tired, deflated woman past child-bearing years whose fertility and creativity are drying up like some old leaf. How long 'til it falls off the tree to float to the ground and become part of the past?

Even today, so many who love me and want to celebrate the remarkable accomplishments of my life (by their standards), who are calling the office or stopping by to say Happy Birthday, are disappointed that they not have the opportunity to do so because I chose to stay home. What do I owe them? What do I owe myself? When is it OK to be selfish? Don't I have the right to simply BE on my day? Just Be – and feel – and sift? I feel so tired. Literally and figuratively.

Timothy calls to say what do you want to do for your birthday? I know he means well. I want to stop crying, to feel hopeful and certain. I want the arrogance of my youth back, the vast horizon of the future to hold nothing but promises of hope. I want to hold my babies once more. I want to know I've been true to myself. I want to stand on a stage and hold people spell-bound by my words. I want my father back, my dog alive. I want peace. I want… I want too many things – too much.

I am undone by my wants.

I am undone.

I am.

Fifty.

Attics, Sheds and Invincibility

"In the winter of my life I saw that there was in me an invincible summer."
—Albert Camus

BRAVING THE DROPPING TEMPERATURES, I went for a walk with a friend last week. We strolled along the little two-lane road that leads to our retreat site at South Lake. I walk this road often in summer, its wide shoulder and infrequent traffic offering a splendid walking trail with unspoiled vistas on which to gaze. The road is sparsely populated and densely wooded so that in the summer the abundant leaves obscure much of what is visible in the winter.

As we walked this well known road I noticed a small ramshackle shed, rusted and beaten by years of winter's wrath. It had obviously been obscured in the summer. We passed it twice on our way – once there, once back – and it drew my attention both times. I found that curious. On the first pass I had thought "How unattractive. I wonder why the owner doesn't clean it up?" On the way back I thought, "It's not unattractive so much as untended." It had stood there for quite some time. A fresh coat of paint would spruce it right up.

The next weekend, I drove to the States to help my sister get a huge project started; she is moving from the home she's lived in for nine years and she's accumulated a lot of stuff. The very notion of packing was overwhelming to her so I offered to come help get the ball rolling. Having moved six times in those same nine years, I have some expertise in the culling process. Her attic seemed most daunting as it contained a lot of unknown stuff crammed into boxes and jammed onto shelves. So we started there. After several hours of pulling out and sorting through and throwing away the fear factor had been cut in half. "It's starting that's the hardest part," she said when we relaxed that evening. "Now that I've begun the process it doesn't feel quite so overwhelming."

Now isn't that just like that rusty old shed?

When things are going our way – the summer of our lives – when we are full of hope and possibilities, energy and activities, we don't see our sheds. It's easy to forget about what's obscured by the full foliage. But when the leaves of those trees fall to the ground in winter, when things aren't going as we planned, when life throws us a curveball (like a big move), all of a sudden, as if from nowhere, an attic ignored or a shed forgotten becomes visible and we feel blind-sided and beaten by the knowledge of its existence and the effort now required to attend to it.

Perhaps that is one purpose of winter, to reveal to us those places in our lives that now require our attention. We do not clean up what we do not see. And when we do sort through and clean out the stuff we no longer want it evokes a sense of completion and pride. "Look what I accomplished. I have cleaned out my shed."

I think it is the human condition that we often choose to examine our metaphoric attics and sheds in wintertime. True mastery is a willingness to walk the woods in summer, cleaning up the sheds as we go, content to greet the rough times as a natural part in the cycle of life. I believe it is this *willingness* coupled with courageous determination that builds an unshakeable self-confidence and a certain kind of invincibility – an imperviousness to winter's wrath – that is born of knowledge.

This winter, go through your attic, walk your own woods. Explore your sheds. Find their beauty, their gifts to you. Bless them and give them a fresh coat of paint. That way, even in summer when they may be obscured from view, you'll be aware of their existence, you'll know what's inside and you'll know you can always find what you're looking for. You'll not feel ashamed of any shed on your property and no one will be able to find anything incriminating in your attic because you've cleaned it up and tossed away what's no longer needed. You know what's inside. *That's* when fear steps aside and we realize there's nothing left to fear except, as Winston Churchill said, fear itself.

And *that's* invincibility.

Heroes, Eagles and Miracle-Makers

"As always, the rest is up to you."
—Peter Gabriel

PEOPLE WE LABEL HEROES DISPLAY characteristics we admire. They can be quiet, unassuming, or larger than life. We might know them personally or only know *of* them. Their common denominator is this: they invite us to see our own possibilities. Through their eyes we catch a glimpse our own greatness. In their choices, we redefine our own. Heroes evoke hope.

One of my heroes is Peter Gabriel. His life and lyrics inspire me. His choice to leave Genesis in the 70's, to stay true to his own voice in the face of criticism, to integrate various indigenous forms of instruments and rhythms into his own music in order to promote world unity, remind me of greater considerations than my own myopic concerns. When I listen to his music I am lifted up and out of a narrow way of seeing and invited to expand the horizon of my limited perspective. His concert in Toronto the summer of 2003 was the finest performance of any kind I have ever witnessed. I left full of hope and a sense of potential for the world. That's what heroes do – inspire us.

Sometimes our heroes accomplish what others perceive as miracles. They accomplish extraordinary things though they began, as do we all, as ordinary people: Gandhi, Jesus, Buddha, Martin Luther King, Jr., Mohammed, Thich Nhat Hahn, M. Scott Peck, Carl Jung. They didn't set out to become great; they simply followed a path – one step at a time – that eventually led them there. When they heard the call, they answered *"yes."* Peter Gabriel writes about this in his hit single of the 80's:

> *"Climbing up on Solsbury Hill I could see the city lights.*
> *Wind was blowing, time stood still, eagle flew out of the night.*
> *He was something to observe. Came in close, I heard a voice.*
> *Standing stretching every nerve, I had to listen, had no choice.*
> *I did not believe the information, just had to trust imagination.*
> *My heart going boom, boom, boom –*
> *"Son," he said, "Grab your things I've come to take you home."*

At the end of the song, during which he wrestles with the potential fall-out of his decision, ("My friends will think I am a nut," and "Open doors will soon be shut,") he finally spreads his wings and jumps with a joyful refrain, "I'll show them what the smile on my face means. 'Hey' I said, 'You can keep my things and come and take me home.'"

Could greatness be as simple as recognizing our individual eagle within and responding to its invitation with a resounding "Yes"? To give by choice the gift it is we came to deliver?

I think it's terrifying to stand at the edge, to look the eagle in the eye, to know you'll never be the same regardless of the answer. But to turn your back on the invitation is to squander life in the bitter wasteland of "what ifs." It is more terrifying than surrendering to the *yes* of personal greatness, no matter the scale of its display. While the choice may be simple it is not easy. With it comes the clear understanding that it will cost us. Ultimately, whatever we choose, it *will* cost us our life.

My husband and I watched the biography of John F. Kennedy last night. The famous line from his inaugural address reminded me that national thinking is no longer enough. The time for global thinking is here: the eradication of political barricades and cultural barriers, of religious divisions and social demarcations, of medical arrogance and legal madness. The eagle is more difficult to see through the haze of worry, more difficult to hear through the static of anxiety. The learned ability to turn down the noise of our frenzied world and to find the balance within provides the soil that grows greatness. It happens one decision at a time.

All of us have greatness within us. All of us are potential miracle-makers. Let us redefine the word to include the everyday kind: the warm smile, the understanding word, the considerate gesture. These smaller choices enable us to tap into the individual power of "yes," creating a collective force that can build new bridges over the barriers of fearful human separation. *Today, ask not what the world can do for you. Ask what you can do for your world.*

Your eagle calls.

Tragedies, Trials and Triumphs

"Show me a hero and I will write you a tragedy."
—F. Scott Fitzgerald

JUST AS AN ACORN SPROUTS an oak tree, so tragedies breed heroes. The people I admire have chosen to trust through their trials, have chosen to overcome their limitations or obstacles, and have emerged from their struggles as men and women of character and conviction. As fire tempers steel, so too our individual characters – indeed, our destinies – are often determined by the choices we make in response to our disappointments. We can let the sorrows of our life to become our reason for relinquishing our dreams or our catalyst for continuing to persevere.

I have a lot of heroes, people who either took a stand for something or who overcame great odds. One of them is my eldest son, Michael. He has been one of my greatest teachers and at twenty-two he's already experienced his fair share of tragedies.

Michael experienced another loss this holiday season. He was to have taken off for Denver on December 29th, with his dog, all his belongings and two of his buddies. He had an apartment and he had been accepted into the graphic arts school in

Colorado. He was so excited about this move and a chance to start over – free from the stigmas of the past! The moving truck had already pulled out a day earlier. Everything was in place. It all looked so perfect on paper. It was a fresh start to a life checkered with disappointments and defeats.

Four years ago Mike got a DUI. He's completed his probation. He's done his community service. There was only the paperwork to be signed by his probation officer. But Mike left it until the last minute. And at the last minute, his probation office *didn't* sign the papers and he was not legally allowed to leave the state and head for Colorado. A hard lesson, indeed.

He called me from Baltimore, sobbing. It may have been the hardest phone call I've ever received with the exception of the news of my father's untimely death. This call, too, felt very death-like. The loss of hope feels like a death. In the middle of leading the Trust Program, I was given the opportunity to really walk my own talk and to back it up by staying really present with my participants. So I did what I could to try to give my son a glimmer of hope at the end of a now blackened tunnel and lift him from the despair threatening to engulf him.

The next day he called again and sounded better than I expected. We talked about the opportunity to rise above this challenge by turning around and really facing his past and his participation in its creation. He had written a beautiful letter to the judge in charge of his case and took it to the courthouse hoping she would allow him to leave the state in time to start classes on January 12th. I urged him to hand that letter off with a prayer for a timely and positive resolution to this situation, to hand it off with gratitude *for* the future, not fear *of* it.

And then I let him go. I let my son free-fall from the plane of fear (what *should* have, *could* have, *would* have been, if only....) into the arms of truth (the way it is, is the way it is). And then I jumped out after him and found myself floating in a cloud of peace the likes of which I have rarely experienced thus far in my life, especially when it comes to the welfare of my sons.

New Year's Day I drove my youngest sister to the Ottawa airport for her flight home to Chicago. She had assisted the Trust Program that completed on New Year's Eve. Driving back to South Lake on a sunny day, the first day of a brand new year, I thought of Michael and gave thanks. I couldn't seem to find the place I usually land when free-falling, the place of worry and worst case scenarios. I felt *happy*. I felt *calm*. I had a deep sense of knowing everything was not just going to work out as it *should*, but rather that it was *being* worked out and all that worrying would do would be to block that natural process. I couldn't help thinking, *what's wrong with me? Why don't I feel upset?*

That night, I had a long conversation with another sister who is a parish priest in Pennsylvania. I didn't really want to get into Mike's story, I didn't really want to have the conversation at all, not because I didn't welcome the opportunity, I just didn't want to repeat some of my old patterns of dumping on family. And I was tired after leading the program and ready to shut down. But when she called I answered the phone and eventually I did tell her this recent chapter in Mike's story, without emotion, without tears. We tried closing the conversation several times, to no avail.

Finally, I suddenly asked if she would write a letter on Mike's behalf to the judge. You're a priest, I said, and the role carries credibility. Internally it felt as though I had just been jolted awake. Something was happening, I just didn't know what. Of course, she replied, but how do I know where to send it? I gave her the judge's name, which I had gotten from my son. There was a long pause. My sister repeated the name. Yes, I said. To which she replied, if this is the same person, I think I graduated High School with her.

At that moment everything in me resonated with the magnificent, marvelous, miracle we call life. At that precise moment, regardless of the outcome, I understood on an experiential level something I've been preaching and teaching for years. It's not enough to say the words. It's not enough to back it up with actions that appear to be in alignment with the words. We must *believe*, at our very core, the truth of trusting and the only way that translates in human experience is to *feel* it in our heart, to give thanks for the way it is, not wishing it was different.

A wise woman (my mother) once said something to me I've repeated often through the years. During my divorce a decade ago she said, "Remember, dear, that love is a verb before it's a noun. Love," she continued, "is a choice, not a feeling. Making that choice *creates* the feeling."

The same is true for trust. Choosing to trust despite the situation creates the *feeling* most people I know want more than anything in the world – internal peace and balance – and it becomes easier and more natural to free-fall more often and more gracefully without landing in a swamp.

My sister *did* write a letter. Turns out, the judge *is* a former classmate. What are the odds? A coincidence? I cannot believe that. I do not believe it.

It is Wednesday, January 7, 2004. Michael had hoped to know the outcome by now. So had I, not only for Mike, but for the wonderful way in which I could prove my words to you who read them each month. What a tidy ending it would have been! But I am free falling, you see. No parachute any longer. No bargaining or pleading with God, no planning and projecting, just trust, beautiful, elegant, mysterious trust.

As you make your resolutions this New Year, as you plan out your dreams and the steps you'll take to achieve them, remember this: though it may be the view for which we long from the top of the mountain, it is the climb up that strengthens us. And we are not alone in that climb. An apparent "no" sometimes means "not yet." Rest in that knowledge and calm will creep into your heart as surely as sunlight spilling over the horizon at daybreak.

Mike is supposed to start classes on Monday. Should he not be able to do so, the consequences are severe – no schooling, no home, and he'd owe his father $8,000 US, that portion of tuition already paid. Mike is prepared, now, to accept whatever the ruling. He understands, intellectually, that the Universe apparently wants him "paid up" before he goes to Denver. Emotionally, he hopes this setback is the last bill. Either way, he says, he's ready to face his future head on because he is no longer trying to out-run his past.

And that makes him a hero in my book.

Trials Terminated

"The most satisfying and ecstatic faith is almost purely agnostic. It trusts absolutely without professing to know it all."
—H. L. Mencken

LAST MONTH I SHARED THE story of my son's disappointment concerning his scheduled move to Denver. The January newsletter reflected my experience of trusting the process. I heard from many of you who were touched or inspired by Michael's story and interested in learning the outcome.

The newsletter was sent out electronically on Wednesday, January 7th. Each day that week, Mike had contacted the courthouse to see if the judge had reviewed his file and rendered a verdict. Each day he was told, no, nothing's been posted yet, and to call back the next day. So he waited, and hoped, and thought – a lot – since the television (interestingly) wouldn't work. His father and brother were away on a ski vacation and all his friends thought he had already left town so Mike left it that way, preferring the solitude suddenly available to him.

On Friday afternoon, at the last possible moment (4:00 PM), Michael finally went to the courthouse prepared to present his case in person, banging on whatever doors might be necessary. By the time he arrived the judge had entered her ruling into the computer. Her judgment was summed up in two words: *Probation terminated*. Not only was Michael now free to leave the state, but also his probation period, originally to be over the end of May 2004, was now complete. Of the various possibilities available on the scales of justice, this was the best possible outcome. Michael's debt is paid in full.

When he called to share the good news I informed him he had been the topic of the newsletter and that a lot of people had sent their support during the week. He wanted to see what I had written so I sent him an e-mail. He read it before he left. Later that evening he called me from the road with his computer, clothes and canine (Koda, a large Husky) crammed into the car and asked that I send a personal thank you to all the people who had prayed for him.

Every mother knows the sound of emotion in her child's throat. Mike was genuinely moved by the knowledge that so many people cared for him and the knowledge that he might be an agent for change in others as he stood strong in his own life. The relief, the joy, the sense of connection came together and he choked out, "Tell everyone I said Thanks, Mom." "I will, honey." "No, *really*, Mom, I mean it. Say *Thanks* – for everything." He arrived in Denver safe and sound Sunday morning and appeared on campus Monday morning committed to starting a new life.

It's a wonderful story. I love the way it all turned out so perfectly, that I have the opportunity to share good news, that my son is safe and happy. But more importantly, *most* importantly, it is *this* aspect I am pleased to share with you: I felt no differently *after* I heard the joyous news on Friday afternoon than *before* I had heard it. There was no cloud of doom through which the sun suddenly burst forth. There was no waiting to find out the ruling before being able to fully enjoy my week. I had been living inside the bubble of trust, a safe and warm place.

Was it *nice* to know Mike was on his way? Yes. He is my son. Was it a *relief* to get the news? Not really. He is his own man now. And that's the most important part. The absence of the feeling of "relief" indicated that I held no expectations, no "*Please* God, please, please, *please,* let him be allowed to go." Praying for a specific outcome is about fear, control and short sightedness. I had prayed that no matter what it would all work together for good. I prayed that Mike would see and learn whatever opportunities for growth were being presented him. I gave thanks for the way it was all the way through, because the way it *was,* was perfect.

I learned some very important lessons from this experience. I learned what trust in the face of perceived calamities looks and feels like. It's like sitting calmly in the center of a cyclone, watching life swirl about you and feeling a gentle curiosity and profound gratitude. It's like putting in your order at a favourite restaurant knowing your meal will be prepared exactly as you would want, even if you're trying a new dish. It means living with daily delight. It means no more excuses for lack of a sense of passion or purpose or your own potential.

I do not profess to fully understand the myriad layers and subtleties involved in this experience of trusting, I only know that the experience of free-falling can go one of two ways: either you jump out of the plane and are frightened the whole way down that your parachute won't open, or that you'll go *splat* on the landing; or you jump out of that plane with sheer abandon, trusting the entire ride. And oh, what a ride! Chances are that not only will your parachute open you'll also find you've grown wings.

Who knows? Maybe Mike would have made it out to Denver

without my absolute belief that all would be well. I just prefer to believe that *my* belief helped *his* belief. Trusting in the midst of personal trials does not necessarily alter the outcomes – it alters our *experience* of those trials. *That's* what changes our lives.

Want to lower your stress level? Try trusting. It's like a Buckley's Cough Syrup for the soul: tastes awful short-term, but works long-term.

Prisons, Promises and Paradise

"Do not seek to have everything that happens to happen as you wish, but wish for everything to happen as it actually does happen, and your life will be serene."
—Dorothy Parker

TUESDAY, MARCH 2, 2004

I sit in front of a large picture window. The sun shines brightly, the sky uncluttered by clouds, and the landscape is snow-covered and pristine in its brilliant whiteness. This is not the snow-covered landscape one finds in the city. Sooty-gray sidewalks do not exist here. It is a visual paradise.

Until Friday, however, emotionally I was in a self-imposed prison. Arriving a week ago, I came here to write. I came to South Lake to focus on completing the first draft of my book and spew forth the raging whirlpool of synthesized data aligned in my head. I am in re-write mode and it's not *half* as much fun as first write flow. It's where the real work begins. Sort of like the difference between *having* a child and *raising* a child.

I promised myself (and my coach) that I would put onto paper a certain number of written words by a certain date. I had made the same promise a few weeks prior, intending to write quite a bit while conducting the Joy Class in Jamaica. It didn't happen. Constant interruptions and a duel focus. I realized that writing and leading a program are mutually exclusive endeavors. Another visual paradise witnessed through eyes with blinders affixed.

So I called another program leader last week to lead the Trust Program so that I could *really* focus on writing. I kept *saying* I would focus. I just didn't *do* it. While I didn't lead the class, I was on site during it and it seemed that each day presented a stream of more interruptions. Friday, feeling stuck and somewhat frustrated I clued into the cause and effect of my situation and decided to release my own arbitrary agenda and relax; *allow* it to happen, not *make* it happen.

Funny thing, I began to notice that the more I focused on what had already been accomplished and less on what had yet *to be* accomplished, the more relaxed I became, the less other people being "in my space" bothered me. The words began to flow. I began counting my blessings and actually *feeling* grateful. I felt unstuck, in the flow, alive, ready to *really* roll as soon as all the participants and team pulled out Sunday afternoon.

Monday morning I got up early, made a cup of coffee and headed to my laptop, excited and ready to work. The newsletter was due (but not yet finished) and I intended to complete it, get it to the office "on time," and then get back to the book. All in the same day.

That was *my* plan. *Life's* plan differed. It was just after 8:00 AM, and the power went out. No storm, no apparent reason for it, but everything in the house went silent. The radio clicked off, the little numbers on digital clocks went black, as did the microwave and coffee maker, the refrigerator stopped its constant low hum, and the heater stopped pumping air. Stayed off all day. Over 1300 homes affected. Never did find out what happened, but on it popped late in the day. Good thing – the house was getting rather chilly.

The point is this: I rolled with it. Apparently, yesterday was *not* a writing day. It was a listening day, a day to hear truth from the deeper regions of silence offered in the absence of electrically motored mechanical objects. Days when everything seems to go wrong are often invitations from the Universe to stop and listen. Refusal to accept those invitations is not a good enough reason to complain about not having attended the party.

There's a saying I like: Expect the best. Accept the rest. That attitude and a little gratitude will take you a long way.

Maybe even all the way to paradise.

One Good Question

"We make our world significant by the courage of our
questions and by the depth of our answers."
—Carl Sagan

ALBERT EINSTEIN WAS ONCE ASKED the following question during an interview: "What is the single greatest question mankind is here to address?" Pausing, Einstein replied by reframing the journalist's query. "I believe the most important question," he responded slowly, "that *each* man or woman must answer for him or herself is, 'Is the universe a friendly place?'"

Einstein's question is still a most important one and a great place to start in a search for confidence, understanding, and internal balance. Your answer to it will define all your subsequent questions – and all your answers. If you believe the universe is a friendly, safe place, a place with an underlying order to it, that belief structure sprouts corollary beliefs which produce one set of psychological, emotional, and physical responses.

If you believe the universe is *not* a friendly place, that the world is a dangerous and untrustworthy place where your life means very little in the grand scheme of things, then your behavioural and emotional patterns will reflect that belief set. It all starts with a single question.

"Do you believe the universe is a friendly place?"

Your response to that question is a *primary* choice and an *initial* building block – the cornerstone – in a personal belief structure that determines who you are and what you will become.

Sounds simple enough. Just say "yes" (as it were) and your life will become rosy? Hardly. Most of us have plenty of evidence stored in our brain vault to negate the notion of the world being a safe place. Watch the news. Read a newspaper. The world is *not* a safe place. Yet, if a child is raised in a loving environment, at two they are the most trusting people on the face of the planet. Generally at three, coinciding (interestingly) with children entering preschool, the world often becomes a less safe place and belief structures begin shape shifting and taking root. Comparisons begin, labels are applied, opinions formed, attitudes shaped, ultimately solidifying by the age of fifteen into a way of viewing the world that predetermines our choices. Those choices – usually small, incremental stepping-stones – predict our results. We end up wondering what went askew, where did we lose our sense of self, our focus, our inner compass?

Too often our questions are formed in the wake of crisis. What should I do? How can I repair this situation? When is life going to get easier? Eventually, tired of drama-driven learning, you can come closer to "living your way" into discovering your own answers by asking new kinds of questions: "Who am I really? What do I stand for? What kind of legacy do I want to leave? What brings meaning to my life? How can I enrich my life and the lives of those I love?"

Playwright Eugene Ionesco said, "It's not the answer that enlightens but the question." Sometimes it only takes one good question to start unwinding a tangled ball of yarn. One good question can unlock passion in the heart and energy in the soul. One good question can open windows of wisdom and doors of decisions. One good question can unblock emotional confusion and release spiritual potential.

One of my favourites is from the poet Rilke:

"Be patient with all the questions in your heart and try to love the questions themselves. Do not search for the answers, which could not be given to you now – because you could not live them now. And the point is to live everything. So live the questions now. That way, one day, without even noticing it, you will gradually live your way into the answers."

There are answers to be had. Rarely will they stem from your head. Keep listening, though. You will most likely find your way back to what you once knew by heart – when you were three.

Sundials, Shining and Sharing

"Hide not your talents, they for use were made.
What's a sundial in the shade?"
—Benjamin Franklin

THERE'S AN OLD CHILDREN'S SONG, sung at many a church camp that goes like this: "This little light of mine, I'm gonna' let it shine." You know the words. We all know the words. We agree *intellectually* that letting our light shine is a "good" thing, something we "ought" to do, but *emotionally* we're afraid we're not good enough, that we'll mess it up somehow. We are *so* hard on ourselves. That old perfectionist perspective: I can only be valuable and contributory if I'm perfect.

I'll let you in on a little secret: if you wait for something to be perfect, you will wait a very long time. Some people wait their whole lives waiting for the best circumstances or enough money or more training or the right moment. The waiting game, as Dr. Seuss says, is "a most useless place." It's a place of confusion, condemnation and comparison.

Some people are gifted with voices that sound like angels when they sing and yet they shy away from requests to sing for others, so afraid are they of making a mistake or of being heard. Others can see something and draw it perfectly on a piece of paper or canvas, but they keep those pictures hidden away in a drawer. Some people are able to string words together on the page like luminous pearls, but keep them in cases, afraid of environmental damage should they be worn for the world to see. Others are naturally compassionate and beat themselves up for not being "thicker-skinned." Some people have a gift for listening but chastise themselves for not talking more. Still others are skilled laborers and wish they were "educated." It seems to me that life is the best educator around. Too bad we don't give degrees from *her* school.

Some of us don't really believe – way down deep – that our particular light is worth being glimpsed by others. Or we may not feel we know what our light is, so how can we share it? Some believe they don't even *have* a light inside them. These beliefs are built on the comparison game. "My ability/talent/skill/gift isn't as good/bright/noticeable or pleasing as *that* person's." This attitude is not only self-defeating, it's inaccurate. It's a bit like saying apples are better than oranges, or that mashed potatoes are better than boiled carrots, or that skiing is better than ice skating, or that singing is better than painting. Or oak trees are better than maples, or that roses are more valuable than lilies, or sunshine is more worthy than rain. As humans we'd have a difficult time attempting to live without sunshine *or* rain. We may like one or the other better, and we require them both to live.

Consider this perspective. Imagine that your body represents all the skills and talents of the world. We'll have your right hand represent musicians while your left is all the mothers of the world. Your right foot is all the athletes of the world, and your left will represent accountants. Your eyes represent doctors, your ears are teachers. You get the idea. Now, choose one piece of you that's better, more important than all the others. Would you want to live without your feet? Your eyes? Your hands? Your ears? Of course not. Yet that is essentially what you're saying when you deny not only the people around you, but also *yourself* of the gift of *you*.

We *all* make a difference, whether we're waiting, working, or wishing. We make a contribution to the whole body of this world by our very existence. Take your sundial out of the shade this month and place it proudly for the rest of the world to see.

It will tell you this: it's your time to shine.

On Family Patterns and Community Living

> "Being in a family is a little like having a
> bowling alley inside your head."
> —Martin Mull

EVERY YEAR MY FAMILY GATHERS at our family cottage on the shores of Hill Island in the heart of the 1000 Islands. We adore the place; it's a slice of paradise removed from mainland living. It represents fun and sun, rest and reading, our youth and the father who built and nurtured it.

Every year we tumble from our cars on the Canadian mainland in Rockport, bounce in boats across the river to unload all our stuff and attempt to claim a bed in a home built for a single family. There are the six grown siblings and various spouses with a total of nine children, assorted friends, seven dogs and one cat. The kitchen has two burners, no stove and one fridge. (Mice rule the shelves until the cat arrives.) It's pandemonium when we're all there.

Every year we sigh and roll our eyes and get cross with one another until the rhythm sets in and we remember we're not CEO's at the cottage – we're family. Usually the day before people start leaving we start adjusting. And every year we make plans to gather again already oblivious of the uncomfortable transition time required to adjust to community living.

Carl Jung observed that relationships are like crucibles in which our character defects rise to the top. How astute was this man? A few moments into arrival I feel sucked back into behavioural patterns evidenced long ago as eldest sibling to six brothers and sisters! The difference, as I reminded myself over the weekend while in the bosom of my beloved family, is that I am aware of those patterns now. Acutely aware. Well, aware of *most* of them. Even as my character defects rise and my emotions kick in I remind myself I am not who I was when twelve years old. Ah, what a practice ground is family!

There's a mantra I sometimes remember to repeat to myself when I feel challenged: "This is an opportunity to demonstrate my current level of self-mastery." I say it several times to myself before opening my mouth to speak in response to a question or stinging remark. It helps me pick a less caustic reply. I also remind myself that these people with whom I have shared such a long history really do love me even if they don't always understand or agree with me.

And I remind myself that I am a big girl now. I am capable of making different choices that honour those I love. I suspect the swift return to interpersonal patterns of "how it used to be" is about connecting, not controlling. We use the tools available to us. As I remind participants in my programs, "The burden of responsibility for change in your relationships is on your shoulders now because you are the ones with the information. You now have new tools. Go and share them with your loved ones. Don't correct *them* – lead them by correcting yourself." Can that feel unfair sometimes? You bet. Do it anyway. The pay-off is worth it.

Perhaps family is God's way of reminding us that in the grand scheme of things no one is more or less important than anyone else and that people are generally doing the best they know how with the information they have available to them.

Tonight I return to the island, the three-hour drive a perk of living in Toronto. There will be even more family members there than last weekend. My brother the doctor is conducting his annual symphony, a multi-hour seven-course meal with seven accompanying wines appropriate to each course. My brother loves big productions and results and sharing all kinds of information whether the listener wants to know about it or not... *Oh no! Who does that remind me of?*

"This is an opportunity to demonstrate my current level of self-mastery!"

On Landscapes, Leadership and Compasses

> "Nothing is sudden. Not an explosion – planned, timed, wired carefully – not the burst door. Just as the earth invisibly prepares its cataclysms, so history is the gradual instant."
> —Anne Michaels, author

I TRAVELED TO DENVER LAST week to visit my eldest son, Michael, now twenty-three years of age. Having large pockets of time available while waiting for my flights in various airports, I read a novel, a rare occurrence, entitled *Fugitive Pieces*, breathtakingly beautifully written by Anne Michaels. I copied at least twenty different quotes from this rare gem into my journal, but it is the one above I pondered during my time with my son.

I happened to read the *New York Times* as well (not quite so beautiful a read) on the way there and then again on the way back. On Wednesday August 25, 2004, the front page headlines read: "*A Trail Leads to Rumsfield*" and in the column next to it: "*Rules on Inmates Need Overhaul, Abuse Panel Says.*" Underneath ran the words: "*Chain of Command Faulted*" and finally, "*In Wake of

Abu Ghraib, Military is Urged to Use a 'Moral' Compass."

A moral compass? Now? The abuse of prisoners at the prison in Iraq is simply the needle; the direction it points reflects the nature of the leadership under whose tenure the abuse occurred.

On my return trip Sunday the 29th, I found two articles of particular interest (in light of the Anne Michaels quote) especially as they related to the idea of a 'moral' compass – and my own mothering. I had just spent four days of uninterrupted, one-on-one time with my son, something I've rarely had the opportunity to do, and I observed myself really noticing the man he's become, not just the child whose landscape I helped form. The first article discussed the history of the human genome (DNA). It read in part,

> "Genes do not act singly, but in complex networks: intermeshing biochemical pathways that form a tangled web of development. Thus a change in one pathway can ramify through many others, so that one mutation can, in the end, have many effects. It is not just the genes themselves that form this network. ...so-called 'junk DNA' (apparently functionless, repetitious sequences of DNA) forms the landscape within which genes operate."

This landscape within which our genes "live" shapes the functioning of our human development. To use an analogy, would the New York Yankees have developed the same way if they hailed from Cleveland? Hardly, it's quite a different landscape. Would *you* have developed into who you are without your life history – *as it is* – all of it, the good, the bad, *and* the ugly?

The second piece was a lead-in for a couple of book reviews

by Emily Barton. She writes:

> "It's one of the most cherished American myths: that in the vast sprawl of our varied landscape, personal destinies can unfold without limits. Here, we like to believe, people are free to shape the places they live in, not the other way round. But in reality a particular setting can have a deep and subtle influence over the fate of its inhabitants – a reality that, paradoxically, is best explored in fiction."

Perhaps we explore that reality so well in fiction because it's so darn difficult in real life. Our lives, our histories, our landscapes, are so riddled with pock-marks and war-wounds that we want to move on – to change the landscape quickly and clearly and cleanly. But it doesn't work that way. It takes time. History evolves. And it is created everyday.

What happened at Abu Ghraib was a gradual instant. In a society that demands immediate results, I suspect that the US will have a rather messy time attempting to recreate a moral compass quickly enough to offset the horrendous indications at Abu Ghraib: that the US military leaders strayed from 'due north' long ago. Lest we forget, compasses are magnetic in nature. The needle responds to the most powerful force in its field.

As I watched my son make small, daily choices during my stay with him, I was reminded that while I may have contributed to some of his topographical pain, I also contributed much of what I value in him: he is kind, sensitive, creative and caring. He knows his 'due north.' His internal compass operates pretty accurately and he is now able to navigate life's rocky shorelines. His landscape included an off-site mother since he was fifteen. Did my choice undermine or uphold the formation of a foundation on which he can rely? After eight years (and countless guilt-trips), I am able to say (finally) yes, yes, I am satisfied with the evidence of the ways in which I coloured the landscape of Mike's life. I am pleased with the compass he now carries.

    Its creation was a gradual instant.

    But then, its due north has always been love.

An Expert Source

"Love is all you need."
—The Beatles

SPEAKING WITH A FRENCH-CANADIAN FRIEND recently she remarked that she wished the French language had more than one word to express "affection for." The French verb "aimer" means to like or love depending on the context in which it is used. I had thought the English language restrictive; at least we have two words to express fondness.

Just what is "love?" It may be all we need, but what, exactly does it look like? And feel like? Uncovering answers to those questions is a lifetime endeavor. And I think that our understanding of love changes as we age and our perspective reflects additional life experience. Still, there are some constants and they are the subtleties for which all of us search whether we know it or not.

Sometimes love is about care giving. Sometimes it is about guidance. Other times it means letting go. Still others demand hanging on. Sometimes love demands sacrificing, other times it requires selfishness. Sometimes it's about tolerance, or timeliness, or toughness. Most times it's about patience and often it's about providing or protecting, but very rarely is it about purchasing.

Yesterday was "Black Friday" in the U.S., the largest shopping day of the calendar year. Having begun my professional career as a buyer I remember well the long work weeks between Thanksgiving and Christmas. It is estimated that 220 billion dollars will be spent in North America on gifts this holiday season. That's two hundred and twenty BILLION dollars and much of it will be spent on things we don't *really* need to give to some people we don't *really* like with money we don't *really* have. For what? To prove we care?

Today I cleaned out a bunch of old e-mails and came across a bit of wisdom from some people who know a lot about the subject of real love. They haven't yet unlearned what we all once knew: that love is the stuff between the lines, the everyday kindnesses and the glue that binds us one to another. It may look and feel a lot of different ways, but the glue is the same and not a bit of it has a price tag attached.

A group of four to eight year olds were asked this question: "What does love mean?" The answers they gave were broader and deeper than anyone could have imagined. Across the board these youngsters gave remarkably astute summaries – snippets – of the nature of real love.

There was some advice: "If you want to learn to love better, you should start with a friend who you hate." Pretty good advice. And there were lots of examples from their families:

- "Love is when my mommy makes coffee for my daddy and she takes a sip before giving it to him, to make sure the taste is OK."
- "Love is when mommy gives daddy the best piece of chicken."
- "When my grandma got arthritis, she couldn't bend over

and paint her toenails anymore. So my grandpa does it for her now all the time, even when his hands got arthritis too. That's love."

That's also profoundly astute. The author is six years old. Was I ever that wise?

Children learn by watching and sometimes by listening – but mostly by reading between the lines. The children I know are experts at extrapolating truth from the most basic of life experiences – and from the grey areas with which so many adults have difficulty. The following observation by a seven year old struck me most: "Love is what's in the room with you at Christmas," he said, "if you stop opening presents and listen."

Maybe then we'll get what we need most this year: a little more love and a lot less stuff.

Compassion in Crisis

"Every adversity, every failure, every heartache carries with it the seed of an equal or greater benefit."
—Napoleon Hill

THE TSUNAMI STRUCK WITH THE stealthy cunning of a lioness stalking her prey: throaty roar heard and felt simultaneously, too late for escape. Locals living on the shores of the Indian Ocean as well as families vacationing over the holidays were swept away indiscriminately. This is our generation's single greatest natural catastrophe. The death toll, which may never truly be known, is now estimated at over 140,000 men, women and children. The images being broadcast over the airwaves – the terrible destruction, the grief-stricken faces, the sad, scared eyes of the survivors – are haunting in their depiction of horrendous hurt and indescribable loss.

How are we as North Americans, so physically far-removed from the epicenter of this tragedy, supposed to internalize and react to so random an amputation of humanity? A donation is only a click away by computer, but does that satisfy our need to make sense of the sudden elimination of so many of our spiritual relatives?

Sometimes the only way I can begin to absorb the macro

events in the world is by choosing to view them through a micro filter. I had a conversation with my mother over the holidays during which I compared the Caribbean hurricanes to my brother-in-law's raging chest cold. Imagining the world as one "body" it stands to reason that "illness" would erupt occasionally. The body is in a constant state of self-repair. The average adult human being produces about 250,000 cancer cells each day. The majority of healthy humans have well-operating immune systems that attack and wipe out those cancer cells each day. Occasionally, though, imbalance erupts.

On New Year's Day I watched a CBC special "David Suzuki Speaks." Suzuki, arguably Canada's greatest living scientist and ecology activist, is also a remarkably engaging speaker. His enthusiasm for his topic – the interconnectedness of our planet's ecosystems – is infectious, instilling in his listeners a heart-felt interest to do something about the terrible legacy we are leaving our children. Our children may be better educated, they may have all the advantages money can buy, but we continue to rob them each day of the earth's precious natural resources through water and air pollution, fossil fuel depletion and soil erosion.

My brother-in-law's coughing, sneezing and wheezing are the overt symptoms of his body's fight against a respiratory infection. With the rapid rise in the frequency of natural disasters I cannot help but wonder if the Earth is not now manifesting her own healing symptoms. Could she be fighting her own festering infections: too much consumerism and not enough conservationism; too much concrete and not enough trees; too much knowledge with too little understanding; too many people but too little connection; too many machines and too few conversations; too many conveniences with too few convictions?

Times of crisis command our full focus. They demand our complete, undivided attention, so much so that we have no room to ponder our petty problems. Crises invite us to alter our current thinking, to change our current choices. They call forth from the human spirit that which defines us as a race: our ability, indeed our willingness, to survive and to rise again after a fall. Hope does spring eternal in the human heart and carries with it the courage and perseverance to rise to new levels. Perhaps, as I continue to hope, we will ride this tsunami wave of calamity until it becomes a wave of compassion carrying humanity to a new shore of unity and health.

It is never too late to play a part in the creation of a New Year — or a new world.

The Ultimate Form of Self-Mastery

"Human behavior flows from three main sources: desire, emotion, and knowledge."
—Plato

"Your intellect may be confused but your emotions will never lie to you."
—Roger Ebert

THERE ARE MANY FORMS OF self-mastery – physical, intellectual, financial – but the greatest form, I believe, is emotional self-mastery. Personal and professional advancement demands an awareness of emotions, not a suppression of them.

Stories abound of world-class athletes with adolescent attitudes, successful business people with short fuses, as well as mind-blowing geniuses who can't carry on a conversation. Sometimes the greatest leaders do not have the best bodies, the biggest bank accounts or the quickest quips. Rather they have mastered their emotions. That does *not* mean they don't have them. It does *not* mean they don't display them. It *does* mean that they are able to choose when, where and how much. They control their emotions

– their emotions don't control them. This requires a desire for increased self-knowledge, understanding and acceptance.

There are basically two sources of emotion: love (gratitude) and fear (anxiety). Think of them as coal and wood, two types of fuel, both of which create fire. The smoke they produce we call "feelings." According to psychologists there are five basic feelings: mad, sad, glad, lonely and scared. All other feelings are derivatives of these five. Today, therapists include shame as a sixth feeling in the same way intuition is considered the sixth sense.

Everyone has feelings, all kinds of feelings. Some we like: tenderness, kindness, joy, delight, awe, inspiration. It's the ones we don't like, the ones we don't deal with that can cause health problems when left to fester. These unresolved negative feelings collect over time – like soot – clogging the internal "airwaves" of our bodies with busy signals. Eventually this creates dysfunctional patterns with behavioural, emotional and physical symptoms.

Feelings differ from emotions in that they are *the products* of emotion. Imagine a rocket ship and think of it this way: the big ball of fiery power at lift-off is the *emotion* (love or fear) that launches the ship; your *thoughts* are the guidance system that sets the rocket on a particular trajectory and where the rocket lands is called a *feeling*.

The eyes may be the window of the soul but feelings are its voice. They comprise a "language." They provide internal feedback; the more you stray off-track, the more severe your feelings become. Feelings are not created in a vacuum. Neither are they to be dismissed. Recognize them for what they are – a guidance system designed *by* you, *for* you – an invitation to learn more *about* you.

When we are able to decipher what the feeling is attempting to tell us, a need to change, tell our self the truth, apologize, declare our position, trust our self, or step up and speak out, we will find we experience less negative feelings and more positive ones. Like children starved for attention, we'll settle for negative attention over none at all.

Give yourself a little positive attention by listening to your feelings. They only want to help you.

They not only tell the truth, they are the purveyors of peace.

The Freedom of Dancing with Death

"The fear of death follows from the fear of life.
A man who lives fully is prepared to die at any time."
—Mark Twain

WHEN DEATH CUTS IN ON the dance floor he is a seductive and commanding partner. I know the feel of his hand on the small of my back. Firm and confident, he determines the rhythm and pace of the steps: one can do nothing but follow.

Last month I had the opportunity to dance with death, consciously yet completely ignorant of what was happening to me. I was helpless in the arms of this partner. It was, for one day, a waltz I shall not forget. I learned the depth of my own fortitude, found the strength of my own will. And I learned what it feels like to lose one's mind: there is certain lucidity in the center of lunacy. I have new compassion for and understanding of the mentally ill.

On Tuesday March 8th, 2005 my husband and I were overcome with carbon monoxide fumes from a faulty furnace exhaust. We were apparently unconscious for four days. On what I now know to be Saturday, March 12th, for some unknown reason I awakened at 8:30 AM. I wandered about the house, wondering why my husband was passed out on the bathroom floor, why when I walked I crashed into the walls, why I was so thirsty. The data did not compute. Everything simply *was*. It didn't require an explanation. I was in and out of consciousness all day. Eventually (twelve hours later) I managed to dial the phone. It took forty minutes to align ten digits correctly in my mind and transpose them to the keypad. The person I called recognized my incoherence and notified the paramedics.

Dialing that phone was perhaps the most difficult thing I've ever done in that it required a focused force of sheer will the likes of which I had never experienced before. As the carbon monoxide seeps into the bloodstream the poison affects the frontal lobe of the neo-cortex impairing a person's ability to reason, to communicate and to exert one's will. Well meaning people say "why didn't you dial 911?" Had I been able to think in such a logical manner I would not have been suffering from the insidious effects of this toxic substance.

The paramedics said that another hour or two and it would have been lights out – permanently. People said "thank god you're alive!" Frankly, for a full week I wasn't so sure it was a good thing at all. After the initial shock of the incident itself and the recovery in hospital (hyperbaric treatments) wore off, the reality of the event and the memories I had of it hit me square in the face and I was overwhelmed with emotions swarming inside me, erupting in ugly, horrible waves of torrential tears and angry outbursts. Though irrational it was nonetheless very real.

For ten days the storm raged as I fought to sear the frayed nerve endings of my irrevocably altered life. I allowed it to happen. I understood the value in acknowledging the feelings of violation, loss, confusion, anxiety, guilt, resentment and frustration (to mention just a few). And the value in *feeling* them, instead of "hushing" them like errant children misbehaving in public. They needed to be *heard* in order to heal.

I said to a friend, "Suppose an orthopedic surgeon requires a hip replacement. All the intellectual information in his head about what's actually going on in his body doesn't help him much as he's trying to re-learn how to walk. Knowledge may dispel *fear*, but it doesn't dispel *pain*."

I was excruciatingly aware of what I was going through. And then the skies cleared and the sun poked its head out and things started to fall into place. I took a look at those feelings and the reasons behind them. I translated and found the meaning and the sense of it, enough so to be able to move on. Unfortunately, that means moving on from our once lovely apartment, moving on from certain relationships I once deemed important, and moving on from half-truths I once sold myself for the sake of harmony.

Last month's editorial began: "There are many forms of self-mastery – physical, intellectual, financial – but the greatest form, I believe, is emotional self-mastery. Personal and professional advancement demands an awareness of emotions, not a suppression of them." I wrote that from my desk at home, on Tuesday morning, March 1st. I also know, now, that I am accurate with the statement, indeed the entire commentary. I've had the opportunity to live it, viscerally, in quite an intense and accelerated fashion. In hindsight I might have picked a slightly less dramatic method of testing my theory.

In a recent phone conversation with my mother she attempted to sum up what she thought I was saying to her. "You're no longer afraid of dying," she remarked. I replied, "Afraid of dying?

I haven't been afraid of dying since I was three! Mom, I'm no longer afraid of *living*."

I understand the difference now. Dancing with death makes some things very clear. It reminds me of the line from *Bobby Magee*, "Freedom's just another word for nothing left to lose." When you're no longer afraid of *losing* something (a promotion, someone's approval, a relationship, money, your pride, position, power, control, your life, or anything else) then you're also no longer afraid of really *living* either.

It's the ultimate personal freedom.

Finding the Chuckle Inside

"You can turn painful situations around through laughter.
If you can find humour in anything, even poverty,
you can survive it."
—Bill Cosby

IF WE STAND STILL LONG enough we can witness the spectrums of life running away from center: the rich are getting richer, the poor, poorer; the forests, fewer, the waters more polluted; people more protected, relationships maintained electronically. The polarities are accelerating. If you feel torn in opposite directions most of the time – between the office and home, friends and family, clients and co-workers – consider yourself normal. It is no longer *if* you'll experience the shifting sands, it is a matter of *when*.

When is now.

The paradigms of the past are crumbling before our eyes. Big businesses are imploding, churches collapsing, leaders toppling, politicians floundering (Ok, so *that's* not new!). Ethics is overtaking Power in the race for survival. And now IBM is giving away access to patented material! They are seeing the potential in (gasp!) *sharing* information. For *free*!

Very little is certain or solid these days. It is a time of massive and momentous change with a new framework for participation in life erupting from the fissured foundations of our former beliefs. In these days of increasing turmoil we are invited into a new way of being. We are being invited to demonstrate acceptance, flexibility and resilience. This demands a sense of humour. Not *being* funny; being able to find the "funny" in a given situation, especially the uncomfortable ones.

I've learned a bit about the healing power of humour in the last little while. My husband and I continue to recover from our brush with death in March. Six weeks post-accident we are able to tally the total impact of the carbon monoxide poisoning more clearly. Some of the after-effects are subtle but nonetheless bothersome: a tingling in the fingers, loss of balance, slower left-right brain communication. During a recent corporate class I meant to say "anathema;" it came out "enema." We all chuckled. These things happen more often these days. If I don't find the chuckle in it all, I might feel very sorry for myself indeed. I could compare myself to who I used to be instead of exploring who it is I am now.

Our individual *response* to the pull of polarities in our lives determines our *experience* of them. If we greet them with resistance and resentment, we will continue to experience resistance and resentment. If we greet them as a natural part of the rapidly altering kaleidoscope of our accelerating evolution we will experience a sense of peace and calm, both of which seem to be in short supply in the world today.

If you cannot find the humour in a situation, you still have something to learn from it. Repeat after me: "It's all good!"

Practice repeating until the phrase pops from your mouth whenever you feel challenged by an unplanned, unwanted set of circumstances. If you have to crash land, pick the Humour Highway; it is the most forgiving landing strip available.

When you can laugh at it, you can live with it.

Mechanical Dependency

> "The most likely way for the world to be destroyed, most experts agree, is by accident. That's where we come in; we're the computer professionals. We cause accidents."
> —Nathaniel Borenstein, author of *Programming as if People Mattered*

LACKING INSPIRATION FOR A COMMENTARY topic this month, I did what I usually do; waited to be tapped on the shoulder and provided direction. I try to do that these days; let the universe steer my ship. I like the notion of working in harmony with a greater force. Yes, I like that notion a lot. Being a team player. Working in harmony with the universe. How lovely.

Rested and ready with coffee in hand, I arrived at my desk Monday morning prepared to be steered somewhere – *any*where – that would take me to the shore of a worthwhile topic. I turned on some gentle music. I opened my e-mail and sank into the day. Nothing like having all the pieces in place. Suddenly, my computer began flashing alarming messages at me, the gist of which was basically "Turn me off NOW!" the implication being that failure to comply might activate all kinds of nasty side-effects, not to mention the end of the world as I know it.

My computer and I have a militaristic relationship: it gives orders and I follow them. Funny, even my husband avoids issuing orders knowing they a) won't work and b) could cost him. But my computer is the boss of me so instead of writing this column I ended up packing up my laptop and toting it to the local Future Shop for diagnosis and repair. Apparently the fan has died and further use could (gasp!) cause the mother board to melt. They need to order the part and then do the repairs and it could take two weeks.

The potential loss of my laptop for so long a period stopped me cold. You would have thought that I had just been told I needed an operation and would be unable to move for a month. My whole life is trapped in that hunk of metal. What about all those unanswered e-mails? My ponderous files? (Yes, they're backed up – it is *not* the same.) I stood there, mouth open, staring straight at the defenseless young man behind the counter and I began sputtering. Small noises escaped my lips, whimpering sounds they were; having never heard them before I could barely translate them for *myself*, let alone the poor man behind the counter who stood there watching me go into shock. I was not emotionally prepared for such a swift and lengthy parting. Like a mother grieving the guilty verdict, I felt like I was supposed to say good bye to my loved one, right now, and the words wouldn't form.

When did I become so dependent upon this silly square hunk of gray metal? It shows me no affection, no respect and certainly has no sense of humour whatsoever. (In that regard it ranks well behind the cat, who in terms of showing me respect ranks well behind the dog.) While this particular model has provided two years of consistent service, others in the office go whacko, for no good reason, causing headaches on a regular basis. For something that is logic driven (so they tell me) computers appear highly random and illogical to me.

Isaac Asimov, author of *I, Robot*, said "I do not fear computers. I fear the lack of them." At this moment so do I. And *that* frightens me. I can live without a microwave or dishwasher. I can function without a car or phone or even a cell phone. I can find fulfillment without a television or DVD player. But, as was made plain to me today, the notion of going a couple of weeks without my laptop causes me to cringe. (Cringe? Freeze!)

The truth is staring me in the face: I am addicted to my computer. I am leashed to my laptop. Where's the Twelve-step program for that? Of course I've become dependent on my PC, it's the way business is conducted in these days of instant everything. Or is it just evolution? Have we as a society, as a culture, become so machine dependent that an implosion cannot be far around the corner? That's the ultimate nature of evolution. Implosion follows explosion. With the rise in internet banking, on-line shopping and e-mail as our preferred form of communication (as well as research) what is one to do when one's life-line to the world is suddenly snipped?

Personally, I thought I handled it all very well. It was as I returned to the office feeling unmoored that I drifted up onto solid ground. After being wrapped in blankets to ward off the trembling, I came out of shock with resounding clarity. It was time to return to human contact, to personal conversations and to snail mail! It was time to cut the machine ties that bind! And it was time to write a not-so-serious-and-far-from-politically-profound newsletter.

Seems the universe does provide direction. And it certainly

has a sense of humour.
   I can't wait to see if my laptop returns with either one.

The Point in Between

"It takes two to speak the truth – one to speak,
and another to hear."
—Henry David Thoreau

WHEN PEOPLE SEEK SOLUTIONS TO personal or professional issues they often perceive the problems as being outside themselves: the situation, the circumstances, the event, management, family, or "the other guy." Asserting a point of view from the only perspective they truly understand – their own – they generally present it as though it is the truth. They say things like, "The fact of the matter is..." or "Well, the truth is you're wrong!"

Truth is a tricky thing. It's elusive and highly subjective. British philosopher A. N. Whitehead once remarked, "There are no whole truths; all truths are half truths." Like a wedding, it just depends on which side of the aisle you sit.

A client contacted me recently to explain a shift in her employment. She had quit. Having connected with me in a class she had attended and aware that I know her employer well, she wrote to give me "her side of the story." I suspect she was concerned that I might hear a different version from my friend. Well, of course I'll hear a different version from my friend! If he even mentions it, no matter what he says it won't be the truth, no more than his former employee's version is the truth. It may have been the truth for each of them individually but collectively the truth lies somewhere in between.

I hear different versions of "the truth" everyday. So do you. For example, there's my truth and there's my husband's truth. There's my son's truth and his brother's truth. There is your boss's truth and then there's *his* boss's truth. On and on it goes. It is estimated that at least 90% of all conflict results from perceptual differences; I see it one way, you see it another. Then we interpret the data, come to our individual conclusions and lo and behold! The results differ and we proclaim each other wrong.

And none of it is true unless the two (or more) people involved in a misunderstanding find that place where the various interpretations overlap. That meeting ground, the point in between, is the place where accuracy can be discerned and connection established. Somewhere in between the various versions of an incident or set of circumstances lies the real truth. The trick is in understanding that to uncover it one must be willing to release all desire to be right.

What? Hold on now, I didn't say that means you're *wrong*. It just means you're not *right*. There's a difference. That difference is to be found in the place I call the point in between. That point is entirely objective and dispassionate. That's the thing about truth; it doesn't play favourites.

The next time you're sure you're right about something and someone else is sure you're wrong ask yourself if it really matters on what side of the church you sit at a wedding? Could the truth, the reason for the gathering, be walking down the center aisle, somewhere in between?

If you look closely, it will be the one dressed in white.

Laws of Life

MAY 9, 2005

Dear Michael,

Happy Day after Mother's Day. Thanks again for your call yesterday. I don't care when or where or why you call or how you sound when you do; I adore the sound of your voice. I just want to put into writing some of what we talked about by phone, not only as a way to summarize the conversation but also in order to expand on certain notions we discussed. While the sound of the human voice connects and comforts, sometimes the printed word can serve to reinforce concepts more clearly and consistently.

You and I are transitioning into an adult relationship. My intent in writing to you is to offer partnership, an available ear to transition into that place of personal strength. No one can do it alone. Human beings are built for relationship. We are hard-wired for love even though we fight it every step of the way. The first step is forgiveness, because harboring the hurts of the past only blocks the flow of goods sailing into port. No one loves completely who does not forgive completely.

Forgiveness is a very complex concept. That's why so many

people, myself included, take so long to exercise it. Sometimes forgiveness happens in a blink of an eye, but more often it is an incremental process, not a linear, one-time-does-it thing, so it can take some time. Or none at all. Every day we have the choice to greet circumstances fearfully or gratefully. Every day we have the choice to forgive.

As I said yesterday, you and I are sensitive to the subtle energies around us. We pick up on what others are feeling. Sometimes this can boost us; sometimes it drags us down. I wish I could hold you, comfort you as you deal with the theft of your car and tell you things will all get better and everything will work out and here's the plan. I cannot. It is time now for you to decide that plan. No one can help you define what you want. Others might listen, ask clarifying questions, offer input, but you alone choose. That's the most exciting thing about life. You get to choose. It's like you're sitting in a restaurant, starving, reading the menu over and over while the waiter stands ready with pen and pad. You don't get to eat unless you place your order.

The world is moving faster and people (in general) are accumulating more stuff. We think we need more — more money, more clothes, a better car, a bigger house — in order to survive. We don't. What we need is less stuff in order to thrive. This goes against all our logic when we look around us, yet it is a Law of Life and one worth exploring. With less stuff comes less worry. With less worry comes less stress.

There are Laws of Life, universal laws. These differ from manmade laws in that they are not subject to our limited logic or our sense of safety. These Laws of Life are about love and creation. They exist because they exist. It's not within our realm of rights or power to question or fight them. There is no higher court to which we can appeal when we feel the sting of having violated one of these Laws. I don't much care for rules – neither do you – but at fifty I finally decided to stop beating my head against this brick wall.

For example, if you go to England, they drive on the left side of the road instead of the right as Americans do. Let's say you visit and rent a car while there in order to go sight seeing. Would you attempt to drive on the right? No. You'd be flattened by on-coming traffic. Would you attempt to get them to change their law in order for you to feel comfortable while driving there? I doubt it. Rather a waste of time.

So why would you want to drive against the universal traffic pattern? You don't stand a chance. That's what I meant about the connection between your car having been stolen and not having communicated with your father yet that you're dropping out of school; when we don't deal with what we know we should already have addressed, the universe has a way of upping the ante in order to motivate us. That's one interpretation of what's happened. You said you'd tell him of your decision to drop out of college before Easter. You wanted to write it in a letter and I thought that would be a good idea as well. A month later you haven't sent the letter, probably because you didn't want to deal with the consequences. Since you hadn't followed through on your intention, the universe decided to yell at you a bit to get your attention. Kind of like people: we generally get yelled at when we haven't been listening. It's one of the Laws. Here are some others.

Perspective Predicts Reality. Reality is malleable.

I asked you to consider your artist's talent at perspective drawing. Where you to stand as you draw something determines how it will appear on the page. If you stand directly in front of a house and draw it, it would appear two dimensional, flat and lifeless. Walk to a corner and now draw the house and it would appear three dimensional, perspective adding depth to the picture on the page. It is the same with our circumstances. By taking one step to the left or the right, our perspective changes and the way we "see" what's in front of us changes, too.

Right now you're looking straight at the loss of your car and seeing only one perspective. Things appear flat and lifeless in your reality as a result. You said to me, "but it is my reality, Mom! I don't have a car!" You're correct of course. The loss of your vehicle is real. And so is your fear. It is real because you give it life with your focus on it.

This situation, at this time, could be interpreted (drawn on paper) in a variety of ways. It could be that unconsciously you're ready to cut all financial connections with your father and claim your personal freedom. That's one perspective. It could be that you've set it up to overcome the odds – again – because you love underdogs and the sense of triumph that comes with giving anything your best shot. That's another perspective. It could be both of those. Or neither. Think of it as turning a big lump of clay on the wheel: one little extra pressure in a certain spot creates a different shape, a different groove.

No matter how we end up depicting on the page what we're drawing in life, it continues to exist at angles we did not commit to paper. There are an infinite number of ways to interpret anything we draw. Likewise, there are an infinite number of ways to interpret any moment in time. The least effective and most disempowering one is wondering why it had to happen to you. Someday you might figure it out. Maybe you won't. The best thing to do is to feel what you feel — for a little while — and then move on. Get angry, then get over it. "This has happened in my life. So what? Now what?"

Yoda said, "The Force both obeys and commands." When we choose the place of personal power through ownership of its existence, the Force **obeys** us; when we whine and complain and ignore its existence, the Force **commands** us. That's why some people seem to be luckier than others.

Your Thoughts are Alive

Your reality is determined by your thoughts, your feelings and the choices you make in response to the events of your life.

Let me suggest that the active ingredient in life is love and the active ingredient in love is trust. How are you supposed to "love" this stupid, highly inconvenient event in your life? It is no small thing to have your car stolen. The only thing that will assist you is to trust that there is a reason for all of this, even if you can not discern it. Just like you did a year and a half ago when you wanted to go to Denver. You trusted then. Trust now. It works.

Your Feelings are Fuel

They are the children of Your Thoughts. What do you want to feed on? Fear or Freedom? Because that's the choice: you either fuel your fears or your dreams. You get to pick.

Your Power Ends Where Your Fear Begins

Just like driving, you can only move in forward or reverse, not both at the same time. Imagine that you are driving a car with one foot on the accelerator and the other foot on the brake. How far would you actually advance? Not far.

That's enough. I got carried away there for awhile — you know how

I enjoy my soapbox…and you know, when I'm dead and gone you'll be glad to have these words.

I love you.
More than more.
Mom

The World of One

"If you look without, the world of the many exists; if you look within, then the world of one [exists]. If you go outside you may achieve much but you will miss the one. And that one is the very center; if you miss it you have missed all."
—From *The Mustard Seed*, by Osho, Indian Mystic

LAST WEEK MY HUSBAND AND I traveled to Chicago to see U2 perform. It was the week *after* they played four shows in Toronto during September 2005, a rather ironic footnote, but it was a family reunion, or more accurately put, a sibling reunion with a few spouses (and one ex) thrown in for good measure. Originally planned as a way for the six of us to reconnect beyond the summer cottage or other traditional holiday meeting grounds, the outing had been initiated by my husband's and my survival of carbon-monoxide poisoning, one brother's recent fiftieth birthday and one sister's upcoming one. Life's too short we decided. Let's do it.

Heather's birthday is September 21st, she loves U2 and they were to play a gig in the windy city on that day, so another sister who lives there asked another brother who "knows people" to get a bunch of tickets for us back in May. He did. The price per ticket was outrageous, compounded by the fact that it was in US dollars

— a scalper's dream. We paid it anyway, the important thing being that it was a once in a lifetime opportunity to declare our love for one another, a recommitment to the foundation of our mutual heritage and an investment in our collective future.

Standing at the concert I glance at my various siblings: my surgeon brother, mouth agape, arms hanging loosely, bopping to the music in his best white man fashion, looking every bit as malleable and open to life as he was when I worshiped him at seventeen; another brother, he who oversees billions in his position as president of a major corporation, sliding down our row offering a pen with which to sign the back of his t-shirt, hands raised in the air, wagging his fanny as he passes in front of us; a sister, jumping up and down while singing along with the Edge's pounding electric guitar chords looking half her forty years; still another, a priest, wagging her head from side to side, eyes half closed, smiling the smile of one who is aware of the moment of grace produced from the fellowship of family, the ultimate and original community of love.

My youngest sister, Jenny, who played hostess to us in her hometown, surprised us with an assortment of brightly coloured T-shirts that she'd had made. The front read "U2" in big block letters and underneath it the word "Cooks," a play on words as it is both a verb *and* our family name. On the back was the word "ONE" and below it "sisters, brothers." We rented a 15 passenger van ("the love van") and made quite a scene on our way to and from the concert. The phrase "can you feel the love?" is now firmly ensconced in our family lexicon, used indiscriminately and without restraint with each other and strangers on the street. Afterwards people stopped and asked where we got the shirts, they wanted to buy one. No can do, we told them. Special shirts. Soon to be enshrined.

Each of us had our struggles actually getting there – business hiccups, missed planes, financial forfeitures – but we had made a commitment to each other and commitment often demands one to re-examine what's truly important. In the aftermath of my own near death experience, inclusion and kindness have stepped to the front of the line shoving logic and pragmatism to the rear.

The last song in the set is One, an anthem of unity, compassion and understanding. Each of us wears on our wrists a white plastic bracelet imprinted with the word. From somewhere to my right a hand reaches out and grabs me. I am pulled into a small circle of six siblings, enveloped by arms that seem to have no owners. We are one. I hear the lines distinctly, "Love is a temple, love the higher law…One life with each other, sisters, brothers; one life but we're not the same. We get to carry each other, carry each other."

In that moment of connection the rest of the world and all its demands fades far from feeling; there is no room for anything other than the oneness, the wholeness, the love. I am transported to a plane I think we were intended to occupy permanently, a place I once glimpsed. The song ends. The cheering soars. From behind comes a tap on my shoulder. Turning around I see a young woman half my age with a look of something – envy? desire? admiration? – in her eyes. "How do I get in your family?" she asks me. Which one? I want to reply. The family before you is a finite set. The family of man is open to all. I smile and say the only thing that can be heard above the roar of the crowd clamoring for an encore: "Love."

The next day Jenny turned on the Oprah show convinced that Bono, the band's prophetic lead singer, would be the guest that day. He wasn't. Chris Rock was on talking about his experience visiting the Katrina flood victims in New Orleans. A film crew had captured Chris in conversation with a seven year old girl, sitting on her father's lap smiling broadly. "Look at this" Chris said as he choked back tears, "she's happy just sitting with her dad." Visibly moved, he shook his head and choked out, "She's got her daddy. She's smiling. Makes me think of my two little girls. Reminds you of what's really important. Family. If you've got your family you've got everything. Everything."

Bono himself couldn't have put it any better.

I have often waxed lyrical on the notion that change begins first in the individual and spreads outward. This is the basis of the work we do corporately. When people stop communicating with their families, when we make the day-to-day routines of survival more important than the once-in-a-lifetime moments – the everyday opportunities that arrive with or without planning – we forfeit the very thing for which we yearn: a sense of connection. When we do it at the office as well, our world begins to wither and our passion for life along with it.

It is somehow even more poignant to have been present with my family of origin during the devastation of Katrina's (and now Rita's) aftermath. As CNN continues to broadcast pictures of New Orleans' missing children I am reminded of the most precious possession of all: the love we choose to generate internally and express externally. It's a choice. It's a commitment.

Returning to Toronto, I visit the grocery store and pick up a few things. After paying for the items, the cashier hands me back some change and the receipt.

"Have a nice day," she intones parrot-like.

On automatic pilot I reply, "You, too," and then realize what I have said. Halting my forward progress out the checkout lane I stop and look directly into her eyes and smile. "You, too," I repeat.

"U2."

A New Paradigm for Performance Improvement

> "Management works in the system;
> leadership works on the system."
> —Stephen Covey

OUR WORLD IS CHANGING AT the speed of light. People are exhausted. Feeling pulled in eight different directions at once we have little time for reflective thinking or self-awareness. We're too busy to make sense of what ails us.

Yet self-observation and understanding is *exactly* what is required in order to address issues at the core of our current stress levels; lack of meaning and purpose and an increasing need for human beings to express themselves creatively, authentically and immediately. The speed of light is working in ways less obvious than the computer or movie screen; *we* are speeding up. Of course our businesses and organizations are speeding up as well! They are comprised of *us*. The collective cannot remain unchanged when critical mass is reached among the individuals who comprise it.

Some large companies are losing their best and brightest to new dreams, dreams that aren't about making more money. They want flexibility and creativity, purpose and meaning. These people are waking up and walking out, seeking radical departures from former lifestyle choices. Financial accrual is less a determining factor to a sense of self-worth and success. More and more employees are making choices that impact their companies' survival.

It's no longer necessarily what you know about business, it's what you know about *yourself* that determines your ability to withstand the demands of the day. Flexibility is no longer a bonus to one's arsenal of personal skills – a necessary component for professional advancement – it's a requirement for survival.

In his newest book, *The Eighth Habit*, Stephen Covey rolls out a well researched, erudite tome aiming to point the business community in a radical new direction: spirituality. In this regard spirituality has to do with meaning, purpose, inclusion and value. Not God in the boardroom, or prayers at meetings. Not internal political policy setting based on religious viewpoint, but rather an awakening to an understanding of the difference between spirituality and religion: all people are spiritual beings, not all are religious. In fact, more and more people define themselves as feeling connected to *something*, just not the God of their childhood church-going upbringing.

Covey notes that the turnstile approach to training and culture assimilation has not worked well within many large organizations. People feel off-balance, off-center, and stressed-out. We feel resentful a lot of the time, anxious most of the time, and tired all of the time. These pervasive and therefore subtle feelings (because we have grown used to them!) undermine our *real* strength, our spiritual strength, which is the very aspect we need most to recognize, support and nourish in order to survive and grow. We must work on our systems in order to heal their symptoms.

This concept is new? Hardly. Many have preached it for many a year. Radical? Yes, in that Mr. Covey carries credibility within the big-business community others who have been a part of this turning may not carry on a global scale, including myself. He is validating the evolution of business leadership to the level it is already being dragged toward by its own people.

Years ago educators talked about IQ (Intelligence Quotient = Intellectual awareness, business knowledge). IQ tests standardized intelligence and quantified our desire to know and our capacity to learn. Later an inclusion of EQ (Emotional Intelligence = Emotional awareness, people knowledge) became part of our paradigm for performance improvement. We recognized the human need to relate to other people; not only do humans desire to know, we desire to *connect*. We are now on the cusp of SQ (Spiritual Intelligence = Spiritual awareness, self knowledge) becoming the defining factor of the truly successful human being, success being defined as one's *experience* of life – one's ability to embrace change, to welcome flux, to thrive in limbo and to laugh through it all.

In this regard, businesses are required to find other kinds of currencies to keep their best and brightest; working from home, off-hours, job-sharing. And some companies *are* making changes, at least those that see the proverbial handwriting on the wall, by providing their people with alternatives to traditional "training" classes that teach models and methods for achieving success. These models fail miserably when tested by real life application in our new speed of light world. Providing learning environments that foster self-*actualization* as well as self-*awareness* is a key in completing the turn that the business community must make in order to survive the next five years of massive upheaval.

There is very little that will ever be the same again. Get used to it. Get on board the change train or step aside, because you might be crushed in the pressing crowd clamoring to join the journey to personal freedom. It is pulling out from the station of today and will arrive at the station of tomorrow within the next few years. Business leaders know this. IBM sees the destination in sight: sharing previously patented intellectual property with the world for free. CI Funds leader, Bill Holland, is talking about lowering customer fees while increasing their transparency. There are many leaders making the same kinds of choices. How evolved of them. How enlightened. How spiritual. *This* is the future.

The future is *now*.

Enter In

In boldness come
The waiting's done.
ENTER IN
Forgiveness holds
More worth than gold
when all you want is to
ENTER IN
Shoulders back
Lift the chin
All of us can
ENTER IN
When we begin
Exchanging
Holding on for setting free

The Value of Transparency

"Destiny is not a matter of chance, it is a matter of choice; it is not a thing to be waited for, it is a thing to be achieved."
—William Jennings Bryan

AMERICAN ARCHITECT PHILIP JOHNSON BUILT himself a glass house in 1949. He did so in the woods of Connecticut, a very nice place to perch oneself if one chooses to live in a glass house, far from those who might throw stones or peer inside.

I find Mr. Johnson's choice to live in a glass house rather remarkable; either to so *value* nature or – equally if not even more startling – so not to *fear* mankind that one would choose a house of floor to ceiling windows throughout. Think about it. Would you feel comfortable with the neighbours (even if only chipmunk and fox) being able to see through *your* walls? Apparently Mr. Johnson was, enough so that he declared himself openly: here I stand – all of me – naked to the world (metaphorically speaking). Rather bold, confident, the kind of person who blazes a trail.

I remember coming across a truism on leadership a while back that went something like this: 'If everyone in the world did exactly what you did each day, would the world be a better place?'

Every time I play computer solitaire the thought haunts me. Now imagine doing whatever it is *you* waste time on in a glass house. Imagine if people knew some of what you consider to be the ugly parts of your character; the questionable decisions, the shameful secrets, the choices made from fear. *Hmm*...Yet I suspect Mr. Johnson was onto something special – some secret formula for happy living – as was Frank Lloyd Wright, both of whom loved their work, saw nature as holy and pretty much didn't care what anyone else thought about them.

"Can you imagine," Mr. Johnson mused during the filmed interview I happened to watch, "being busy and happy doing what you're doing, every day of your life?" Pausing, this elegant elderly man glanced out the floor-to-ceiling glass wall a few feet from where he sat to take in the encompassing woodlands beyond. Turning back toward the journalist he concluded, "Oh, I've had a wonderful life."

Indeed. I suspect those who live without fear of stones being thrown are the freest of the free. Or perhaps it's the being busy and happy doing what you're doing part. Most likely it's a combination of the two. With a little of Mother Nature's handiwork thrown in for good measure.

As 2005 comes to a close and I reflect on what has been a physically taxing, intellectually demanding and emotionally draining year (indeed, the decade!) I have come to this conclusion: destiny is defined daily. Knowing where you want to go is secondary to knowing where you live. And it had better be a glass house if you want to go somewhere important to you since rock throwing is almost guaranteed in today's world. And since there's more danger of glass walls breaking from the *in*side than the *out*side, you might want to bury that rock supply you've been carrying around before entering. At least, that's one of the things I've learned this year.

I think Mr. Johnson's formula is no secret. It is the same formula taught by many wise people: be true to yourself, do work you love, rejuvenate in nature.

And remember to laugh and travel lightly, especially over the holidays.

Leave your rock collection at home.

The Weight of Character

"Reputation is the shell a man discards when he
leaves life for immortality.
His character he takes with him."
—Anon

I SPOKE WITH AN ACQUAINTANCE last month who was unaware of my springtime dance with death. Having grown weary of the back story I shared only the briefest of salient details before surprising myself with a succinct summary: I remarked that perhaps one of the best things to come out of the incident and subsequent road to recovery was to have come face to face with my own character. Later, reflecting on my own words, I wondered how they had escaped my lips so quickly, so easily. Was it even true? Had I confronted my own character? If so, what does that really *mean*?

We say things like, "Oh, she's quite a character," indicating a person of colourful personality, while "He's a man of character" means something quite different. We refer to the character of concepts, wine, artwork and many other inanimate objects. Bill Clinton's presidency was littered with the remains of carnivorous conversations concerning character and cigars. Character changes with context, or does it?

It has been shown that at the moment of death a person loses 21 grams of body weight. Some have posited that this is the "weight" of the soul. Is that soul, or essence, the well-spring from which character pours forth? While integrity, honesty, generosity, compassion, perseverance or forthrightness are component pieces of any character puzzle on a physical plane, I think it comes down to this: character is that part of the individual which knows its own potential. It is that part which urges us onward and invites us to dig deeper and reach higher than we did yesterday. It is the part of us at peace with itself without being complacent.

Charles de Gaulle, former President of France, once said that "a man of character finds a special attractiveness in difficulty, since it is only by coming to grips with difficulty that he can realize his potentialities." Perhaps character is forged in the fires of life's furnace in much the same way as iron becomes steel. Perhaps in our willingness to confront those fires head on we tap into the eternal power inherent in our *essence* (or whatever it is that weighs 21 grams): our character, the steel backbone of our strength. Everyone *has* character. The question becomes, of what *quality* is it? It's an interesting thought to consider in the face of the materialistic mind-set of our modern world. A few years ago another friend of mine decided to begin living her life by her obituary instead of her resume. She wrote herself one and then set out to live it into being. It's working.

I sat down to do the same thing not long ago. It is an interesting exercise to view oneself dispassionately, without the usual self-recrimination for perceived failures or human foibles. I've been to enough funerals to know that even if the person wasn't as well-loved as some, generally only nice things are said. Too bad we find it so difficult to do that for ourselves.

Over time, for the most part, it's the good that's recalled in a life lived. I think that's what character is: the essence that will be remembered most when it fades from physical view. My father could be one son of a gun (she says politely) and sixteen years after his death it is the *good* messages, the best of him, that I remember most, not the catalogued resentments I collected over the years. He died sixteen years ago today and what lingers still is his 21 grams.

Coming face to face with one's character requires peeking inside that miniscule measurement and finding out what lives within. I'm not sure what others will say about me when I'm gone, but I'm getting clearer on what I want to be able to say about myself.

I have a feeling that's the whole point.

In the End: Back to the Beginning

"We must not cease from exploration. And the end of all our exploring will be to arrive where we began and to know the place for the first time."
—T. S. Eliot

TEN YEARS AGO I MOVED to Toronto to begin a new chapter in my life. I left my homeland and my sons to follow a dream. Along the way I stumbled across a few hard earned personal truths and unearthed the blueprint of my calling. I feel very blessed indeed. But I'm no more special or worthy than anyone else. All I did was choose to live, to learn, and to love. That's it.

This book chronicles a stage in my emotional, intellectual and spiritual evolution. That stage was jump-started by my ex-husband's desire to end our marriage in 1992. The night after he told me he wasn't sure he loved me, I experienced what I would call a mystical journey: I was shown my life in review.

I would like to share that story and its after-effects as a way to close out this collection of essays. It represents the alpha and the omega to me, the beginning, the end and the reason why. It is therefore imperative that I include it in this volume, though my heart quickens to think of certain of my corporate clients reading the words that follow: while these stories are known to some, they are also *not* known to many. Not even my brothers, or Andrew. Because I only tell them at the Trust Program.

Now, I'm sharing those stories with you.

And them.

⌒

When I was three and a half years old I nearly drowned. It is my earliest and most vivid memory. Some forty years later I found out why. It was vivid for good reason.

My parents had purchased a small summer cottage and one evening they had guests over. Somehow my younger brother and I had managed to wander away from their watchful eyes. What I remember clearly is sitting on our immense swimming rock which angled down to the slippery water's edge. I was attempting to show my two year old brother how *not* to get too close to the water because he might slip and fall in. Since he didn't yet know how to swim I was quite protective of him and I thought it was important for him to be aware of the potential risks and to remember to wear his life jacket. The facts that I did not yet know how to swim nor was I wearing a life jacket seemed not to be contradictory in the least at the time – I was his big sister. I remember inching my way down to the base of the rock crab-like, knees up in front, hands behind. It was important for my brother to be shown, I thought, because he didn't really use too many words yet and this was critical stuff I was trying to communicate.

Suddenly, my feet slipped on the slick surface. With nothing to grip, my legs straightened and I slid directly, irrevocably towards the water until I was swallowed up by it. I clearly remember thinking, *this isn't really happening, I can stop my sliding body.* But I couldn't. I remember opening my eyes as I sank beneath the surface and shouting, "help!" and seeing air bubbles float up in front of my open eyes. Then I lost consciousness and sank to the bottom of the river six feet below the surface.

Above, my brother sat as still as a stone and stared at the water. I'm guessing at that detail as I didn't actually see him, being unconscious and all, but that's how my father found him moments later, staring at the water.

By now everyone realized we were missing and they were all looking for us. My father ran down to the dock jutting out sideways from the same large rock. Fortunately he had been a lifeguard and world-class swimmer in his teens. He saw my brother sitting on the rock staring at the water and shouted. "Bill, Bill!" Where's your sister? Where's Cindy?" My brother, now a brilliant orthopedic surgeon and far more articulate, pointed at the water and uttered the family-famous words, "Otter, otter," whereupon my father leapt into the river, grabbed me from the bottom, threw me up on the dock and began CPR. Dad got me breathing again and saved me from permanent brain damage. We think.

I mention this event by way of introduction to the following story. This next singular experience, what I call a mystical journey, completely changed the course of my life by clarifying this earliest childhood memory.

⌒

9:00 PM, September 7, 1992. The previous night my husband of fifteen years had come home and declared our marriage over.

He wasn't happy, he didn't think he loved me, he wasn't sure he knew what love was, nor did I, he admonished me, and he wanted out.

I wanted to die.

He had suffered from debilitating episodes of undiagnosed manic-depression for five years. It was terrifying. I became very good at control and expert at denial. I never knew when he'd break down. I walked on eggshells, exploded at my children over anything and generally slid into my own unhealthy ways of coping. When he told me of his decision I was frozen with fear and thought my life was over. Everything by which I measured my self-esteem was soon to walk out the door along with my pension plan. I had an outdated resume, a fragmented identity and no credit rating. I was thirty-nine years old with two small sons and I felt utterly lost.

That night, while my husband talked, I nodded and made all the right noises desperately hanging to some strand of hope and then totally lost it on the phone with my mother while she listened to me sob for three hours. The next morning I had had no sleep and felt like a zombie but managed to put breakfast on the table and get the boys to school all the while thinking *this can't be happening to me.*

Somehow I made it through the day. The boys were in bed. I was awash with thoughts speeding uncontrollably through my head like some emotional rapier, my heart dying a slow death from a thousand cuts as each scenario and painful possibility played out in my mind. I felt caught up in a cyclone spiraling out of control.

I sat on my bed surrounded by various self-help books and a bible. Let me say that I am neither a bible scholar nor a thumper thereof but I went to church and perceived the reality of my life through a Judeo Christian filter. I believed in a God, but no longer the God of my childhood. I had begun to question the foundations of my faith.

At that time I had what I now call a young faith in that it was simplistic, unquestioned and untested. I took much of my childhood church teachings as truth rather than tradition and so my practices reflected that: a lot of black and white thinking and a lot of guilt in particular. I went to church and attended study groups as a young mother not because I found it enriching but because I thought I *ought* to. It was the *right* thing to do. It was important for the children and for me to be seen as an active participant in my community. My upbringing demanded it. My church attendance, at that time, was more a reflection of my need for other people's approval than a desire to deepen my spiritual awareness.

Under stress I would sometimes flip through the pages of my bible, randomly seeking some answer to a current dilemma. The bible would fall open, my eye scanning the errant page looking for a profound response from God himself. I did this with lots of books, not just the bible. As I said, mine was a young faith.

Reclining on my bed, in great emotional pain, my mind raced with wild end-of-my-life scenarios. Once again I reached for the bible and began my search for comfort. The book fell open to Corinthians I Chapter 13. The words may be familiar. They are often used in wedding ceremonies. The first eight verses read as follows:

> "Though I speak in the tongues of men and even angels, but have not love, my speech is nothing more than a

clanging gong or noisy cymbal. And even if I have prophetic powers, and understand all mysteries and all knowledge, but have not love, it does me no good. I may have the faith to move mountains, but if I don't have love, I am nothing. I may give away all I have and deliver my body to death but if I have not love, I gain nothing. Love is patient and kind; love is not jealous or boastful; it is not arrogant or rude. Love does not insist on its own way; it is not irritable or resentful; it does not rejoice at wrong, but rejoices in the truth. Love bears all things, believes all things, hopes all things, endures all things."
I Corinthians 13:1-8

I read those words. Then I read them again. And again. I'd seen and heard them many times but this time I *heard* them. I *ingested* them. I *felt* them. Suddenly I realized that the aspects of love St. Paul described were actions, not feelings. They were choices and I realized in an excruciating flash of self-awareness that I had not made loving choices for much of my life. I had fallen very short of the mark. I couldn't believe what a mess I was in!

But what *was* this thing called love as Paul described it? How could I know if I truly loved my husband? Certainly I had not been happy for quite some time. Had I ever given myself, my husband, or my life my best shot? How can you say you love someone if you're not sure what it even is?

As I sat there dazed, staring straight ahead, it felt as though a conversation was taking place between my shoulders. Like Sylvester as he's about to pounce on Tweety and the "good" Sylvester (with halo) pops onto one shoulder and says "Don't eat the bird," while on the other shoulder the "bad" Sylvester (with horns) urges him to "Eat the bird!" I felt like that — as though I was split in two, talking in circles. I had come completely unmoored. What is love, real love? I thought, and what does it feel like, really?

I closed my bible, sank back into the pillows and a tidal wave of regret sucked me inside a torrential sea of tears. With eyes closed I began crying for all the times I had hurt others, all the times I had been less than I could have been and all the scorecards I had so carefully maintained. How would I ever learn to really love *any*one when *I* was so unlovable? How would I ever know what real love felt like? I had gotten it so wrong!

And *that's* when it happened.

I was taken on a journey. Whisked away — or wished away, perhaps. I still don't know exactly what to call the next twenty-two minutes: near death experience, astral travel, lucid dream or divine encounter. It doesn't matter. I refer to it as my trip to heaven. Let me say that nothing like this had ever occurred for me before. I did not meditate. I did not chant. I was a mainstream Protestant with no thoughts of reincarnation, karma or spiritual guides. Angels were as much as my limited mind would allow and only because the bible said so.

I found myself in a long, dark tunnel moving through time and space. I could feel the hairs on my arm move in the light breeze created as my body flew through this tunnel. In front of me, though unseen, a presence led the way, flashing pictures from my past in front of me all the while. It was like a giant Rolodex of still life photos, beginning in the present and going backwards through time. The images flicked into view one after the other. I was shown times when I'd said or done hurtful things, but the regret over these mistakes – the pain I felt – was not *mine*. Instead I felt the events from the *other* person's perspective. I could feel my sister's pain as I sliced her verbally across the Christmas dinner table after one too many glasses of wine. I felt my friend's embarrassment as I diminished her in front of her peers in order to elevate myself. These were not the carefully catalogued transgressions of my own keeping. These were the slight sins that send the soul into hiding. These were the ones, I realized, that I'd be called to account for at the end of my life. Not the big boo-boo's but the everyday "unkindnesses" that seemed trivial at the time. That seemed too much effort.

This part of the journey, this retrospective of my life in the dark tunnel, was difficult and sad. I cried the cries of a wounded animal facing its own mortality. I felt alone and small and unworthy. I was in a sort of trance and never reached to wipe my face. (When I came out of it my tee shirt was drenched from the unchecked tears flowing down my chin and falling to my chest.) The images came faster and faster as I traveled further back into my own history to memories stored outside my conscious keeping. There were many from about the age of eleven, which I now recognize as the death of my childhood. The pictures flashed faster and faster. They came so fast I could barely keep up when suddenly, I fell out of the bottom of the tunnel and was sucked inside the body of a little three year old child sitting on a large rock, showing her younger brother how not to get too close to the water.

Time stood still. Everything stopped, including my tears.

And there I sat, a thirty-nine year old woman, wife and mother, inside a little girl's body, knees drawn up to her chest, peering over the top. There were red sneakers on my feet. I turned my head and could see my brother sitting well behind me up on the rock. Wearing a lifejacket! I didn't remember *that*! *Hmm... This is interesting*, I thought. I gazed out over the mighty St. Lawrence River. The water was blue. The sun shone. All was quiet. No boats, just stillness. I sat there and waited and wondered.

And then a resonant voice unlike any I had ever heard, a voice of strength and authority, of goodness and clarity, a voice of wisdom that made me want to weep with a deep and distant recognition, pierced the scene and shattered the stillness with a single question:

"*And where else, Cindy, have you been willing to drown yourself in order to save another?*"

I sat trapped in that little girl's body, my adult mind reeling with the implications of the Voice's insight. Something erupted inside me. My God! I had been doing that all my life! With my father, my husband, with friends, jobs, my children, my church! I had been drowning myself for years, in futile attempts to help others! I had to help *myself* first!

As soon as that realization sunk in it was as though the hand of God herself reached into that little body, grabbed the full-grown woman, yanked her out and sent her hurtling into space. This second part of the journey was not so much about going *forward* in time as the first part had been about going *backward*. It was simply going *somewhere else*, neither forward nor backward, just *else*where.

This part of the journey was filled with a sense of complete joy, humor and lightness. I was floating in space. I saw and heard many things, most of which I no longer remember consciously. I do remember however, *understanding* what I saw and heard and laughing, as though I was privy to some inside universal joke.

The sound of my own laughter was muted, outside my self. I felt safe, balanced, connected to *some*thing, though I did not know what was happening or why. I didn't care. It was wonderful to be floating in space and feeling so free and peaceful.

Eventually I entered a place that contained some sort of beings. I say *beings* because they were not *human* per se. Angels? Spirit guides? Aliens? Who knows. I don't feel compelled to define them.

I entered this space (no walls or doors, but a space of some kind) and saw facing me, about fifty feet away, a set of bleachers. On this multi-tiered structure stood a group of beings, two dozen or so, calmly standing at attention. They were angled to my left and looking straight ahead. I could not see them clearly enough to discern facial characteristics, but I could nonetheless tell when they turned their gaze on me. They had no bodies, per se, but seemed to be draped in robes. They did not speak, yet they communicated. From a distance they looked much like a choir awaiting the arrival of the conductor. In the few seconds it took for the rest of the story to unfold, my life would be forever altered, though I did not know it at that time.

I arrived. I saw this assemblage and recognized them as *mine* somehow, my own private cheering section, gathered and awaiting my arrival. They were waiting for *me*. In unison their heads turned and they looked at me. Again, no eyes like human eyes. But they *saw*, and they *knew*. They knew ME, *all* of me. In that instant I grasped in my essence that every ugly, dirty, shameful, horrible thing I had ever thought, said or done was known to them and that all the things I hoped no one would *ever* find out about me were *already* known – to *them*! And NONE of it mattered – the fears, the mistakes, the shame – all of it was calmly, reverently brushed aside with the message "Do not confuse your humanity with who you really are. You are lovable. You are worthy. We love you – as you are." In that instant I knew I had glimpsed my spiritual heritage. In that instant I knew I had been sprung from these beacons of love and I would return to them again upon my physical death. In that instant I wanted to stay. I had never felt so safe, so accepted, so forgiven, so completely and utterly loved.

That one frozen moment is enough for me to choose to believe that I am a cherished child of the universe. The memory still brings tears to my eyes. Such a blink of an eye, so transient, but so indelibly, irrevocably anchored as the lighthouse of my future voyage on a dark and turbulent sea.

A surge of recognition and long-forgotten awareness moved through me and I moved toward this group. I wanted to *stay*, to be with them! But an unseen presence prevented me. This presence (it felt male) was facing me a few steps in front and off to my right. His right shoulder (had there been one to see) would have been across from my right shoulder. And the same voice – *that voice!* – halted me in my tracks:

"And NOW", the Voice roared, "*You KNOW!*"

The words reverberated as though rolling over a bottomless canyon.

"And *now* you *know*...and *now* you *know*... and *now* you *know*..."

The statement was not a casual, "Well, since you asked, here's the answer." Rather the words exploded as an imperative, "Now that you *know*, what will you do about it? You must *do* something with this knowledge."

It was a command. And I knew it.

Glancing at my cheering section, they began to fade from view. I knew that I was not to stay. I had glimpsed something...I knew *some*thing...*and now I know...now I know...I know...what?* It all faded away and I "woke up" in that I became aware of my body, my bed, a wet Tee shirt and a smile on my face.

I came out of my trance with the Voice's last words ringing through my head. As I became more fully aware of my surroundings I remembered the questions that had precipitated my journey. "What is love? What does real love feel like?"

I had my answers. I had been given a great gift, a glimpse into an ultimate personal truth. I had another chance at love. My life *wasn't* over. It was really just beginning. I *wasn't* going to die. All I had to do was learn how to recreate the feelings of acceptance and inclusion I had experienced on my journey and duplicate my heavenly experience here on earth.

And study this *love* thing.

∽

So began my more formal exploration into the nature of love. I read anything with the word "love" in the title or a Ph.D. after the name of the author. I re-entered therapy, attended twelve-step support groups and continued leading experiential learning programs. (I worked a lot of stuff out in public!) My ex-husband and I maintained a civil and caring relationship, though the separation process of any enmeshed couple is a bumpy ride fraught with ample learning opportunities.

I read everything I could about Jesus (my cultural role model), as well as other spiritual leaders i.e. The Dali Lama, Buddha, Confucius, etc. from a wide variety of viewpoints. Having been raised within the framework of the Episcopal Church I knew very little about non-mainstream belief systems. I wanted to know as much as I could about what I *didn't* know. I began questioning most of the simplistic beliefs by which I had lived. And I began to discern some pillars upon which I could build a new foundation for myself.

After years of determined study, steady healing and lots of programs I once again heard from the Voice, which narrowed my focus and made me a promise.

I was in Toronto conducting a five-day experiential learning program in the fall of 1995. One sunny afternoon before the start of that evening's session I sat ensconced on the 23rd floor of the Westin Harbour Castle Hotel over-looking a bay full of sailboats. I was talking on the phone with a lovely lady with whom I had previously co-facilitated a program. She had just suffered her tenth miscarriage. She had also recently turned forty and felt time was running out for her to be able to bear a child. This happily married, beautiful, bright businesswoman wanted a child more than anything else in the world. My phone call had been one of condolence (I, too, had had a miscarriage) and we talked of her feelings of loss and confusion.

I took the risk of asking her a question that would open new territory in an otherwise pleasant professional relationship with personal overtones. I had come to a certain plateau, a comfortable place in the construction of my own belief structure. I had studied and read, watched and listened, talking to anyone I deemed happy, observing, asking them what they believed and why they believed it. I had begun to dig a new foundation for myself. Now divorced, I may have been a new seedling taking root but I knew what I knew. And I knew that this woman's emotional pain required a spiritual lens for any comfort to be found, for any sense to be made of such repeated heart-breaks. This kind of profound disappointment can not be consoled by logic.

"Joan," I said, "may I ask you a question?" (Joan is a pseudonym to protect her privacy)

I took a breath. "Do you believe in a God?" She responded through her tears immediately. "Oh, yes."

I stared out the window as the sailboats sailed around the harbor far below.

I asked, "Do you love this God of yours?"

"Yes," she said quietly.

I replied, "You *love* your god – but do you *trust* him?"

She went silent at the other end of the line. Aware that she and her husband were avid sailors I drew an analogy.

"Joan, you're a sailor, right?"

"Yes…" Her tone was slightly questioning. She knew that I knew this.

"When you guys go out in your boat and the wind shifts, what do you do?" I asked.

"Adjust the sails," she said. She had stopped crying.

"Or change direction?" I added.

"Yeah…" She was listening.

"You depend on the wind for the power to sail your boat. You have faith in it. You trust it. You adjust to it. You don't yell at the wind for blowing the way it blows, do you?" I paused. "Maybe God's the wind, Joan. Maybe it's time to take a look at what God's saying, what your *soul* is saying, and trust it a little more."

"But it's all I've ever wanted," she whimpered, alluding to her desire for a baby.

"Perhaps the desire you have to *parent* a child is actually already happening in the various companies you've guided to new growth. Look at the relationships you have with your employees, your nieces and nephews. They are strong nurturing relationships. You're already parenting, Joan."

As she began to grasp what I was suggesting – the significant difference between loving and trusting – her voice became calmer and stronger. I'm sure we talked a bit longer but that's the part I remember most clearly.

After we finished our conversation, it felt like electricity was pulsing through my body. I was on fire with the sudden awareness of this key distinction between love and trust. I remember dancing all around the room so enlivened was I by the narrowing of my search for the secret ingredient in the concoction called love. I am now, ten years later, more convinced than ever that without the trust muscle, the bone of faith cannot stand and the legs of love cannot walk.

A few days later, I left Toronto and drove back to Baltimore from the Dulles airport. I was *still* alive with this insight. It was all I was thinking about, all I *wanted* to think about! It's dark, it's raining, the windshield wipers are thwacking back and forth and I'm thinking about this *love* thing now channeled through the *trust* thing when suddenly I think, this is a *big* job. If people only knew, could only be told; if they really understood the power of *trusting*, it could change the world! I could help reframe love – reframe the nature and importance of trust as the cornerstone of love – and link self-trust to God-love to other-love. I was going to teach the world to trust. Oh my God! This was *huge*! And then that side of me which belittles the potential for human brilliance interrupted with a scolding self-rebuke: who was I to think I could help change the world for the better? Who did I think I was?

I asked three questions in the next ten seconds. I received three distinct answers which I consider to be spiritual communications. By that I mean that the answer to my questions sprang into my knowing instantly, fully formed, complete with contextual symbolic imagery. Not word by word or a sentence at a time. A paragraph transmitted and received – *fully formed* – in a single second.

Perhaps it sprang from my subconscious, or my higher self, or my guardian angel, or God. Who cares, really, what one calls this kind of connected moment? It simply doesn't matter. Perhaps I imagined it all, but I do not think so. I had been alive with thoughts, hopes, desires and dreams. I was having a great time driving home that night, but I know the difference between the sound and the pace of my own internal chatter and the sound of *that Voice*. There was no breath between the end of the question and the full answer in response. The answers I received and heard through my own belief system were from a higher source. Not my unconscious. Not my own soul. Not my *own* anything.

I felt a wave of unworthiness wash over me as the first question formed. An old pattern. I queried silently, directed to no one in particular. It was simply a corollary thought-form sprung from my tendency to think big. But an answer was *there*, immediately upon the completion of the question itself, on the point of the question mark, without a breath, without a blink, a fully formed response in *that Voice!*

1) **Who am I to think this way?**
    Answer: *"You are as good as any other."*

The tone was impartial, almost dismissive. The response came complete with tableau intact: God's hanging out at the side of a puppy pen just leaning against the wire mesh and grinning. There's a bunch of beautiful Golden Retriever puppies bouncing around in the pen, maybe six weeks old and cute as can be. Here I come walking up admiring the puppies. "Oh, look at the puppies! Aren't they cute?"

"Yup," says God, "they sure are."

"I hear Goldens are good hunting dogs," says I.

"Yup, they're good hunting dogs," says God. This time he nods his head toward the group frolicking at his feet.

"Well, I want me one of these dogs, God," I tell him. "I want the *best* hunting dog." When he looks slightly puzzled I continue.

"I'd like you to pick out the best puppy in the bunch," I tell him.

God tilts his head as he looks at me and then looks at the puppies. He waves his hand over the litter, eyebrows raised quizzically.

"You pick," he says. "Each one is as good as any another."

In other words, they start out perfect. The way they are raised, trained and fed will determine how effective they become as hunting dogs. That part was in my hands. I understood, instantly, that I was just one of six billion "puppies" running around on this planet – no better, no worse than any other, simply "as good as any other." So my second question sprang as a spontaneous follow-up.

2) **Why me?**

Answer: *"You're listening."*

I leaned forward in the driver's seat, clutched the car's steering wheel and felt what I now call the icy shivers of truth run through me. *This was not my voice*! These were not *my* words! What was happening? Was I going crazy? I took a breath and another chance by asking the kind of question I have since come to discover is the least important of all to ask when thinking on a global scale.

3) How will I do it?

Answer: *"I will give you the words when you need them."*

I understood at that moment that I was not to concern myself with *how* anything would unfold and I have since been reassured to learn that only the sane actually doubt their sanity; the truly nuts think they're just fine. That day I made a deal with the Voice and with whatever creative powers exist in the universe. I'd raise the puppy (me) with as much love as I could muster and keep listening as best I could. She (the Ultimate Power Source) would handle the words and the timing. A decade later I consider that promise fulfilled. And I'm still sane. I think.

On the basis of these two distinct mystical experiences was built a new life, a life dedicated to helping people discover how to *really* trust themselves, their decisions and life in general so as to improve their ability to function in the world in a rewarding way. The columns in this volume flowed from that endeavor. Along the way, I learned how to trust myself as I trust in the wisdom of the universe. It was not an easy decade for me, probably wasn't for you either if you're reading these words, but it was a necessary climb and one for which I am now immensely grateful. I have come, finally, to appreciate the climb itself and have relinquished all desires for a better view.

The search is ended.

This past year, while my husband and I continue to recover from our little nap, as we affectionately refer to the carbon monoxide poisoning, I've learned a few things.

I've learned that waking up in the morning is a blessing and noticing a sunset is a bonus. I've learned that time spent in silence is a valuable thing and that being awakened by the sound of a purring cat is a very good way to begin my day.

I've learned that walking instead of riding, listening instead of talking and feeling instead of thinking are indicators of personal progress. I've learned that the less I own, the freer I feel. And I've learned that craving permanence and certainty only serves to block the flow of ever-present energy from the Source of All: permanence is an illusion.

I've learned that people are generally doing the best they can, the best they know how, based on what they know. Mostly, people just want a reason to believe, a reason to hope, a reason to live, a reason to love.

I've learned that in the end the only thing that matters at all, really, *is* love. Of course, that word is so small it fools one into thinking it can be understood, quantified, proved, or even known. I've learned that while it can be recognized and embraced, much like a favourite friend, there is more below the surface than that which we see and touch. There is a whole other life occurring below the skin of the person we hold in our arms, an unseen life of bone and blood, of intellect and emotion, of passion and purpose that can never be fully grasped by anyone other than that individual. I think love's like that: able to be embraced, able to be demonstrated, able to be seen and felt without ever being fully understood or explained. To surrender to the unknowingness of love and the uncertainty of life is, I've learned, the secret to extracting its inherent joy.

I've learned that the relationship one chooses to entertain with the Divine Source of All That Which Is, however you may define that subjective reality, is a most effective methodology when navigating life's maze. Defining one's relationship with a higher source of wisdom and strength is a required field in the computer program for contentment. That single parameter will predetermine the nature and quality of all our human relationships. And the sum total of the quality of those relationships will define our experience of life and ultimately, our destiny. It's what we create, every day, with every choice. Our understanding of the nature of compassion, the essence of love, or the core of existence – each a way of conveying the same message – will determine our resilience, our strength, and our capacity to connect with everyone and thing around us.

I've learned that the Divine is me – *and* you. That's the most important thing of all. *You* are divine. And so is everyone else (remember that!). We all have the power to shift the chicken shit of our life and turn it into nourishing soil, creating beautiful gardens and sharing the harvest with others. Maybe they're little gardens, maybe they're big ones. It doesn't matter. It isn't the *quantity* of lives you may touch. Rather it is the *quality*, the depth of the ones you *do* touch that matters in the end.

Nowadays my notion of God is quite different than it was when I first heard the Voice. A ruthless interest in and a rudimentary understanding of quantum mechanics and the unseen world has forever altered my former naiveté. I doubt I'll be seeing a guy leaning against a puppy pen again anytime soon. At *that* time the location and the players in the tableau of the puppy pen expressed a message in a language with which I was comfortable, my family having raised Golden Retrievers when I was a child. The Mystical Field in which I now place my trust is kind enough to communicate in many ways, in a larger language, if you will. New research in physics, astronomy and the more scientific aspects of the physiology of love has expanded my vision. Now, the many languages of science, medicine, music, geometry, astrology, astronomy, psychology, the holistic arts and visual and performing arts – *all* have their value.

The landscape of life offers to each of us a variety of sights, sounds and symbols. And sometimes some metaphorical shit gets tossed our way on an otherwise regular day. But any point of view, any belief, any perspective, contains a grain of truth, a pearl of promise. All perspectives hold *some* meaning. And some filters are more effective than others in producing a rewarding and meaningful experience of life.

The most effective filtration system includes a belief in the existence of a unified energy field and the notion of personal interaction with this "field" in all moments whether consciously or unconsciously thought, spoken or acted upon. This perspective demands self-reflection as the basis for sound decision-making and contemplative soul searching in the pursuit of spiritual evolvement. It, in particular, challenges the twenty-first century human being even as it offers the most beneficial internal experience of life. *Love thy neighbor as thyself; Heaven is found within.* How are we to balance this attitudinal approach to decision-making with the "good guys finish last" mentality of the business world? Or the internal conflict caused attempting to balance home and family? Or the heart-ache of forsaking one road to travel another? Seeking answers to these kinds of questions sends the searcher on a universal journey comprising the collective mythology of mankind, even as each of us hunts for our individual place within it.

It is in overlapping the various lenses of life that we must crawl to one conclusion above all else: that there is *something* connecting us all one to another in this earthly experience. Call it Love. Call it God. Call it Energy. Call it Source of All or the Universe or the Tao. Call it what ever you wish. But call it *something*. Identify what you believe and *why* you choose to believe it and then *live* it. Your courage will inspire others. Developing a presumption of underlying purpose to all which occurs is the aim: love is the target. This is a mystical mind-set and will aid in the decomposition of your life's daily doo-doo.

We all have landscapes littered with laments. Get over it. And get on with living. Life *can* and *will* become a veritable bumper crop, a harvest of plenty, when you recognize the nourishing value of your *own* chicken shit for the soul; take it, till it, and turn it into super-soil, enriching everything that grows within it.

After a while, you'll not only get used to the smell, you'll actually begin to enjoy it.

Another paradox.

I love that.

Afterward

"We cannot grow spiritually and remain the same.
Understanding that is knowledge.
Believing it is wisdom.
Knowing it is trust."
—Gary Zukov, author of Seat of the Soul

MICHAEL AND KODA RETURNED TO Baltimore in early 2005. Denver just wasn't home. In September 2005, his father and he decided to attend the Trust Program together thereby turning a significant page in our mutual history. Though another facilitator led that program I did, however, drive to the retreat site on the final day of the class in order to greet them when it was over. The memory of Michael's embrace will remain a high point in my life. *Do you understand now, honey? Do you see why I had to leave?* I whispered in his ear as we held each other. *Oh yes, Mom. I get it*, he whispered back. *Did you get what you came for, Mike?* I asked. He replied *I got a whole new life, Mom. A whole new life.*

It was a watershed moment. It was a fresh start, an ending and a beginning, everything wrapped up into one. Six months later he opened his own business, Baytown Designs, specializing in logo development and design work. The cover of this book is an example of his talent. Call him if you could use his expertise.

Andrew graduated from the University of Maryland with a degree in finance in May, 2006. His dad, always generous, flew in various family members, rented a huge limo and carted us all in style to and from the ceremony, hosting a large dinner at Ruth Chris Steakhouse afterwards. I felt proud to have once been his wife and to have birthed our children. Gazing around the room at so many friends and family members gathered to acknowledge our son was an emotional completion: some sort of period was placed on a last sentence of a paragraph in a closing chapter from a dog-eared book. My baby's all grown up. He's traveling Europe as I write this, ten cities in five weeks, his last spell of freedom before moving to San Diego for a new job – with his surf board and golf clubs. He called to touch base. Says Amsterdam was a blur. Don't call him for anything.

And I've been asked to host an internet radio show on www.VoiceAMerica.com on their newly launched Seventh Wave Network. My program will follow John Gray's show (of *Men are from Mars, Women are from Venus* fame) at 9:00 AM Pacific time for an initial thirteen week run on Mondays beginning September 25, 2006. The hour-long show introducing the concepts and healing methodology I call Synthology™ will have a front-end teaching component followed by expert guests in various fields taking calls and questions from the listening audience. Please do call. Noon (EST) on Mondays. Really. Call.

This radio offer materialized out of nowhere in June 2006, just two days after I signed the contract with Trafford Publishers to (finally) publish *Chicken Shift for the Soul.* An initial thirteen week series on Synthology™ – the topic of my next book – coinciding with the publication of *this* book. Makes you wonder, doesn't it?

But then, it's probably all just a coincidence.

Or is it?

Coming from Cynthia Barlow, 2007

SYNTHOLOGY™:
THE STUDY OF WHOLENESS

Introduction

"Soul and body, I suggest, react sympathetically upon each other."
—Aristotle

MANY HAVE FORGOTTEN MUCH OF what most once held as truth: that the physical, emotional and psychological systems of the human orchestra operate in concert with one another and are conducted by the soul. Spiritual wholeness was acknowledged as the foundation for healthy physical functioning long ago. Twenty-five hundred years after Aristotle we are finally getting back to basics; taking care of your health starts by taking care of your heart. The life of the spirit is as important as the life of the mind.

Eating well, exercising properly and getting enough rest are important ingredients in any recipe for wellness. And they alone are not enough. All of us have heard stories of the athlete who's dropped dead of a heart attack ("But he was in such good shape!") while the octogenarian in Italy who smokes unfiltered cigarettes and drinks a bottle of wine every day lives a long and happy life. Why? Certainly environment and genetics play a part; environment can be chosen and we will examine the way in which genetics can be altered over time by re-patterning human emotional response patterns.

Yet, the *first* choice for a new landscape begins by "seeing with new eyes." If you can't find contentment in your own living room or your current job or relationship, you won't find happiness in Paris or in that "better" job or relationship. "There" is no better than "here."

Years ago educators talked about IQ (Intelligence Quotient). IQ tests standardized intelligence and quantified our desire to learn and to *know*. Later an inclusion of EQ (Emotional Intelligence) became part of our paradigm. We recognized the human need to relate to other people; not only do humans desire to know, we desire to *connect*. We are now on the cusp of SQ (Spiritual Intelligence) becoming the defining factor of the truly successful human being, success being defined as one's *experience* of life, not one's bank balance.

Spiritual intelligence does not mean one's familiarity with or adherence to a particular set of religious rules. It *does* mean acknowledging the divinity in all things and all people. It means being able to see *within*. It means developing our sixth sense, our intuition, our "trust" muscle, in order to live the kind of life for which we yearn; a life of internal peace despite external circumstances. Our desire to *believe* and to *belong* to a greater whole sends us searching for a more meaningful experience of our day-to-day existence. That search inevitably leads us back to where we once began: to ourselves and our *chosen* belief structure. Our personal perspectives, thought patterns, emotional responses and spoken words *are* the whole world.

Gandhi once said, "The only tyrant in my life is the still, small voice of truth inside me." This book is an attempt to help you develop a more successful, rewarding life – to untangle yourself – by discerning your inner voice, deciphering your feelings and distilling *your* truth. That will take you inside where, according to every master in recorded history, the kingdom of heaven is to be found. You probably know that already. You probably *accept* that notion *intellectually* or you would not be curious about reading this book. (IQ) You may even have done enough personal development work (not to be confused with "training" classes) to have arrived at the place where you *own* that statement *emotionally*. You may already understand the importance of relationship maintenance, of taking risks in communication by telling the truth, of seeing the world as your own mirror. (EQ)

Now, you have the opportunity to enter the mirror and see yourself and everyone else, not from the outside in, but from the *inside* out. (SQ) When you strip away the slick lies sold for the sake of success and the half-truths harbored for the sake of harmony and stand naked in front of yourself and *your* understanding of God, not the concept confined to a set of rituals or creeds, you will live in the land of ultimate freedom: you will discover you are not only invincible you are also immortal and intrinsically connected to everything and everyone around you. What you do to another, you do to yourself. What you do to yourself, you do to all creation. In this chosen belief structure exist the seeds for a new life – and a new world.

This book is about building a whole new life – for a whole new world.

Right now.

To contact Cynthia Barlow or Constellation Learning, Inc.
please visit:

www.constellationlearning.ca

www.synthology.ca

Or call:

Phone: (416) 694-6223

ISBN 1412096928